"This book shows in detail how the German Nazi regime persecuted Paul Leo, a German Lutheran pastor, because his ancestors were Jews, how this regime put pressure on the church to comply with their insane persecution of everybody remotely Jewish, and how Leo found a second home in Dubuque, Iowa, as a professor at Wartburg Theological Seminary. This most welcome book is meticulously researched and lavishly illustrated. The authors did an excellent job to render this book into English, and it deserves many readers."

—**Hans Schwarz**, professor emeritus of systematic theology, University of Regensburg

"Craig Nessan and Carsten Linden's book about my father brings him to life, weaving his theology into the flow of his remarkable life. Born in the twilight years of the Victorian era into a thoroughly assimilated, educated, solidly middle-class home, he survived Buchenwald to create a whole new life in the United States as a country pastor and a professor of theology. His faith and optimism shine through the text."

—**Monica Leo**, daughter of Paul Leo

"This work brings to life the dramatic story of Paul Leo, a Lutheran pastor who because of his Jewish heritage was forced to flee Nazi Germany. As a pastor and seminary teacher in the United States, he had lasting influence. In this carefully researched and fascinating book, the reader will see above all the thoughtful, faithful Christian. As a pastor and teacher, Leo focused not on his own suffering but on fulfilling his call to ministry."

—**Mary Jane Haemig**, professor emerita of church history, Luther Seminary

"Today, perhaps even more than ever, the Holocaust's unquenchable mandate, 'Never again,' cries out to be heeded. Even those with ears to hear still often ask, 'How could such evil have taken over such an enlightened, scientific, and historically Christian nation?' Condensing Paul Leo's precarious sojourn, Craig Nessan and Carsten Linden narrate at the granular level the 'how's' of these mid-twentieth-century atrocities as well as the struggles of refugees from trauma and terror back then, with truths as pertinent as ever."

—**Gary M. Simpson**, professor emeritus of systematic theology, Luther Seminary

Paul Leo

Paul Leo

Pastor with Jewish Roots
in Flight from Nazism

BY
Craig L. Nessan
AND
Carsten Linden

FOREWORD BY
Victoria J. Barnett

CASCADE *Books* • Eugene, Oregon

PAUL LEO
Pastor with Jewish Roots in Flight from Nazism

Cascade Books
An Imprint of Wipf and Stock Publishers
199 W. 8th Ave., Suite 3
Eugene, OR 97401

www.wipfandstock.com

PAPERBACK ISBN: 978-1-6667-6578-6
HARDCOVER ISBN: 978-1-6667-6579-3
EBOOK ISBN: 978-1-6667-6580-9

Cataloguing-in-Publication data:

Names: Nessan, Craig L., author. | Linden, Carsten, author. | Barnett, Victoria J., foreword.

Title: Paul Leo : pastor with Jewish roots in flight from nazism / by Craig L. Nessan and Carsten Linden ; foreword by Victoria J. Barnett.

Description: Eugene, OR : Cascade Books, 2024 | Includes bibliographical references and indexes.

Identifiers: ISBN 978-1-6667-6578-6 (paperback) | ISBN 978-1-6667-6579-3 (hardcover) | ISBN 978-1-6667-6580-9 (ebook)

Subjects: LCSH: Leo, Paul, 1893–1958. | Lutheran Church—Germany—History—20th century. | Church and state—Germany—History—1933–1945. | Christianity and politics—Lutheran Church—History—20th century. | Christianity and politics—Germany. | Antisemitism—Germany.

Classification: BX4844 .N37 2024 (print) | BX4844 .N37 (ebook)

01/10/24

We are grateful to Uta Timpe-Bautz of the Verlag Traugott Bautz GmbH, Nordhausen, Germany for permission to publish this English translation of *Paul Leo: lutherischer Pastor mit jüdischen Wurzeln* by Carsten Linden and Craig L. Nessan (Nordhausen, 2019).

Those who cannot remember the past are condemned to repeat it.

—George Santayana, *The Life of Reason* (1905)

Contents

Foreword

THE STORY OF THE so-called "non-Ayran" pastors is usually just a footnote in studies of German Protestantism during the Nazi era. Their numbers were small: approximately 90 out of 18,000 clergy in 1933. Although categorized as Jews under Nazi racial laws, most of them did not consider themselves Jewish (many came from families that had converted in the nineteenth century), and they had little or no contact with the Jewish community. Even before the rise of National Socialism, however, they suffered under the pervasive antisemitism and ethno-nationalism of that era, including such attitudes in the church itself. Only with the publication of Wolfgang Gerlach's *And the Witnesses Were Silent: The Confessing Church and the Persecution of the Jews*[1] was there a deeper examination of this group, the Confessing Church's failure to stand by them, and their subsequent fates.

Paul Leo was a unique and complex figure among them. A descendant of the Jewish philosopher Moses Mendelssohn, Leo was a second-generation Christian who studied for the ministry in the wake of the First World War and was ordained in 1922. Like Hans Ehrenberg, another Confessing pastor of Jewish descent, Leo reflected theologically on the relationship between Judaism and Christianity. He took a complicated position that in some ways reflected the antisemitism surrounding him. Arguing in 1933 that

1. University of Nebraska Press, 2000. Translated and edited by Victoria J. Barnett. The German edition was published in 1987.

"Jewish Christians" should have a separate church, Leo wrote: "The descendant of Jewish parents must affirm for himself and to the outside that he belongs to a non-German people, a special people, which according to God's promise shall not perish."[2] The same argument was being made by Protestant nationalists like theologian Gerhard Kittel, a supporter of the new Nazi regime who argued that it was God's will that German Jews (as a "non-German people") should be stripped of their citizenship.

Yet within his church Leo stood opposed to figures like Kittel, and he became involved in the "Osnabrück Circle," an outspoken group of regional Confessing Church pastors who protested the state measures against the church. This made his life even more difficult, for his bishop in the church of Hanover was August Marahrens. Although a critic of the pro-Nazi "German Christian" movement and state interference in church policy, Marahrens supported compromises with the Nazi state (two of his sons were SA-members) and was openly antisemitic even after 1945.

The first chapter in this volume offers a rare, detailed study of what Paul Leo's ministry looked like in Nazi Germany from 1933 to 1938. He wrestled with the theological and personal significance of the Jewish-Christian relationship and the political pressures within German Protestantism. Despite the steady erosion of support from his church hierarchy, he remained dedicated to his congregation and colleagues. Like most pastors affected by the Nazi racial laws, he was targeted in the violence of the November 1938 "Kristallnacht" pogroms, arrested, and sent to Buchenwald concentration camp. Upon his release one month later, he began the difficult process of emigration, which took him to Holland before he was finally able to reach the United States. There the next phase of his life began, first at Western Theological Seminary in Pittsburgh, then as a pastor in Texas, and finally at Wartburg Theological Seminary in Dubuque, Iowa.

As this book illustrates, however, his story did not end in 1938. Craig Nessan's remarkable account of Leo's life in the United States begins with the memories and insights of Leo's widow Eva.

2. Leo, "Denkschrift," 189–96.

Her account relates the extraordinary difficulties confronting refugees fleeing Nazism who wanted to come to the United States (and the equally extraordinary efforts of those Americans who helped them), and the process of beginning a new life in a new country. Leo gave public talks about the situation of the churches in Nazi Germany. In 1950 he was invited to join the faculty at Wartburg, where he soon won the affection and respect of his colleagues and students. The final chapter, which explores Leo's postwar scholarly publications on theologians like Bultmann and New Testament scholarship, offers an invaluable snapshot of the afterlife of the theological conflicts in Nazi Germany.

Paul Leo died suddenly in 1958 while teaching a class on New Testament exegesis. He was only 65. As the publication of this book illustrates, however, he and his widow left a lasting impression on the Wartburg community in Dubuque. This short volume is a rare portrait of a German theologian and pastor who was persecuted under the racial laws of a totalitarian state. It is also a tribute to the longer impact of a theologically thoughtful life.

Victoria J. Barnett

Frank Talbott, Jr. Endowed Visiting Professor
The University of Virginia
Former Director of the Programs on Ethics, Religion, and the Holocaust
United States Holocaust Memorial Museum

Introduction

I FIRST MET EVA Leo when I was a Master of Divinity student at Wartburg Theological Seminary from 1974 to 1978. At that time, I came to know her as a political activist—who introduced me to Tom Harkin and George McGovern among others—and as the artist of exquisite copper works. Eva's artwork decorated many homes and churches, especially among those who came to know her in Dubuque. Later her stunning depictions of the Works of Mercy (Matt 25:31–40) and the prophetic Word of God as a Lamp (Ps 119:105) adorned the Leo Doors at the Seminary, as does the Emmaus resurrection story (Luke 24:30–32) on the walls of the Augusta von Schwartz Refectory.

Toward the end of my studies, I was privileged to learn the story of the Leo family in a more personal way. Eva became my tutor in learning the German language to meet a requirement for the Master of Sacred Theology degree. For these lessons I went to her home where Eva graciously taught me the basics for reading German but even more engaged me in provocative conversations about world affairs. Many of these conversations went on for two hours or longer and I began to learn from her part of the story described in this book. Eva had followed her beloved Paul to the US in his forced exile from Nazi Germany. The Confessing Church and the study of German theology became very real to me in her witness. It was a matter of life and death decisions.

The film by Ken Burns, Lynn Novick, and Sarah Botstein, *The US and the Holocaust* (2022), provides haunting background for this book. The moral ambiguity and often failure of the American response to the catastrophe of the Holocaust is a tale that needs to become widely known. We have lessons to learn in response to the decisions made by American leaders and institutions to the humanitarian disaster that was unfolding in Europe in the 1930s, especially from the refusal to welcome those who were in mortal danger in their German homeland. As a nation that embraces within its idea of democracy the welcome of immigrants, the realities of bigotry against and exclusion of desperate Jewish people provides a cautionary tale.

The message of "never again!" needs to resound from the Holocaust to confront every new form of genocide. Yet the pattern of moral ambiguity and often failure of the American response to homeless immigrants and desperate refugees continues to mar our national character. We hope that the publication of this story can provide inspiration and instruction for a courageous and generous response to the immigrants and refugees seeking sanctuary in our time. The words of George Santayana at the beginning of the most violent of all human centuries still deserves our observance: "Those who cannot remember the past are condemned to repeat it."[1]

It was providential when Carsten Linden, a German historian, first contacted the Wartburg Theological Seminary Archives for information about Paul Leo. His inquiry was brought to my attention and soon we found ourselves engaged in the collaboration that resulted in this monograph, first published in German and now in this revised English edition. German historians have labored diligently to preserve the memories of those persecuted, imprisoned, and murdered by the Nazi regime. Dr. Linden was committed to discovering the facts about the fate of Paul Leo, which are detailed in the narrative of chapter 1. This constitutes a case study that he has been invited to share on many occasions in Germany.

1. Santayana, *Life of Reason*, 284.

On my part, I had returned to Wartburg Theological Seminary as a professor in 1994. I had the great blessing of friendship with Eva Leo during the last years of her life. No one who met Eva can ever forget her spark, wit, and prophetic stance. The story of the Leos—Eva, Paul, and their children—deserves to become widely remembered, not only by those who knew and loved them but by new generations. This book aims to be one vehicle for this intergenerational transmission. Their legacies also have generated initial work on what I am calling the "Leo Project" at Wartburg Theological Seminary. The two central foci of this project are to spread the story of Paul Leo as told in this book and to preserve the witness of Eva Leo, especially as embodied in her artwork. We are deeply grateful for the support of the Leo children—Anne, Christopher, and Monica—in this effort.

The authors express their gratitude to many for their co-labor with us on the completion of this book. First, we are deeply grateful to Victoria J. Barnett, whom I first met as a scholar working at the US Holocaust Memorial Museum, for writing the Foreword. We are also grateful to the many archivists who assisted with the materials documenting our research, particularly Suzanne Dodd, Wartburg Theological Seminary archivist, Professor Susan Ebertz, Director of the Reu Memorial Library, and the staff of the archive at the University of Marburg. In Germany, we are grateful for the assistance of Stephan Bernhardt, pastor at the evangelische-lutherische Inselkirche in Norderney, and Tobias Harjes, metal sculptor in Schwanewede, Lower Saxony. We underscore again our thanks to Uta Timpe-Bautz of the Verlag Traugott Bautz GmbH, Nordhausen, Germany, for permission to publish this English translation. Finally, we are grateful to our colleagues, students, and families for their solidarity and support.

Craig L. Nessan

Wartburg Theological Seminary, Dubuque, Iowa USA
Ordinary Time 2023

Paul Leo (1893–1958)

I

Life Stations in Germany (1893–1939)[1]

Paul Leo was born on January 9, 1893, in Göttingen, Germany, and died on February 10, 1958, in Dubuque, Iowa, USA. From September 17, 1929, until May 18, 1930, he was married to Anna Leo. They had one daughter by the name of Anna. From July 6, 1940, until February 10, 1958, he was married to Eva Leo, and they had two children, Christopher and Monica.[2]

On his mother's side, the Jewish philosopher Moses Mendelsohn belongs to Paul Leo's ancestors, some of whose descendants converted to Christianity. The granddaughter of Moses Mendelsohn, Fanny Hensel (née Mendelsohn-Bartholdy), the

1. Chapter 1 by Carsten Linden, historian. Translated by Hans Schwarz and Craig L. Nessan.

2. Complete names and further biographical details for the Leo family: Paul Friedrich Leo. His first wife was Anna Lina Adolfine Leo (May 29, 1898 to May 18, 1931). Their daughter was Anna Marie Erika Helene Leo (born May 9, 1931). Her first name after emigration became Anne and her married name was Ellis. With Johanna Elisabeth Eva Leo, née Dittrich (December 2, 1901 to April 10, 1998), he had the children Christopher Peregrinus Leo (born July 30, 1941) and Monica Cecilie Leo, whose married name was Jenks (born October 28, 1944). Biographical details are taken from the Landeskirchliches Archiv Hannover, N 147, "Entschädigungssache Paul Leo"; handwritten curriculum vita of Paul Leo of October 9, 1930, Archiv des Kirchenkreises Osnabrück, Personalakte Pastor Leo; *Osnabrücker Tageblatt* (October 20, 1930); and communication by the archives of Wartburg Theological Seminary, Dubuque, Iowa, from February 25, 2013.

composer and pianist, was a Christian. Paul Leo himself was the great grandson of Fanny Hensel.[3] Paul Leo's father, Friedrich Leo, had Jewish ancestors. He was baptized and was a professor of classical philology at the University of Göttingen.[4]

A Christian with Jewish Roots

Paul Leo was baptized as an infant and therefore was Christian. The ways he remained Jewish lie in the eye of the beholder. A modern formulation says that Paul Leo had "Jewish roots."[5] According to Jewish theology, how one belonged to Judaism varied over the course of time. The one constant was that someone who descended from a Jewish mother was in every case a Jew.[6] To this day, mainstream Judaism "determines the Jewish identity of a child by its birth from the Jewish mother."[7]

According to the conservative Jewish view, even a Christian baptism does not change one's belonging to Judaism.[8] Paul Leo wrote about this in 1933: "The descendant of Jewish parents must affirm for himself and to the outside that he belongs to a non-German people, a special people, which according to God's promise shall not perish. This also holds true for the baptized Jew, because even if it is religion which allowed the Jewish people self-preservation with great tenacity, this Jewish ethnicity is not extinguished once one is baptized."[9]

3. Rocker, "Der Umgang der Landeskirche," 32.

4. Friedrich Leo agreed with a colleague to divide the subject. While this colleague, Ulrich von Willamowitz-Moellendorf, then taught classical Greek, Leo taught Latin and thereby became the founder of Latin studies. Friedrich Leo named his first son, Ulrich, after this colleague.

5. "Im Visier der Nazis—Paul Friedrich Leo," flyer of the Kulturgeschichtlichen Museum in Osnabrück for an event on March 1, 2018. Rocker, "Der Umgang der Landeskirche," 32.

6. Oberlaender, *Wir aber sind nicht Fisch und nicht Fleisch*, 14–38.

7. Boeckler, "Das Mutterprinzip," para. 2.

8. Oberlaender, *Wir aber sind nicht Fisch und nicht Fleisch*, 15.

9. Leo, "Denkschrift," 189–96.

Childhood and Youth

Paul Leo grew up with his parents and two older siblings in a middle-class section of Göttingen, which was then called the professors' quarters, since many university professors lived there. He attended the state high school (*Gymnasium*) in Göttingen and graduated there in 1912.

Paul Leo as Youth

Studies

Beginning with the winter semester 1912, Leo enrolled at the Göttingen University to study the subjects of history and German studies, which later changed to Protestant theology. Twice he volunteered as a soldier during World War I but was deemed unfit. To further the study of theology, he transferred to Tübingen University where he attended classes by Karl Heim and Adolf Schlatter. Finally, he moved to Marburg University to study with Otto Heiler and Rudolf Bultmann. In spring 1919 he concluded his studies by completing the first theological exam, but then continued for approximately one more year at Marburg to write his inaugural dissertation.[10] With a few other students at Marburg in the winter semester 1918–19, he reactivated the fraternity, *Akademische Vereinigung* (Academic Union), which recently had been dissolved.[11]

In the church of Hanover applicants for a pastorate were usually assigned, at the completion of their studies, to serve as vicar with the pastor of a congregation to gain practical education. As an alternative, there could be further education at a *Predigerseminar* (Preachers Seminary). This provided a period of further theological studies but with less practical experience. The decision between these two alternatives was usually determined by the grades in the first theological exam. Paul Leo had received the highest marks in his first theological exam and therefore was placed into the Preachers Seminary Erichsburg, where he studied for eighteen months in 1921–22 and graduated with his second theological exam.[12] On August 22, 1922, he was ordained in Aurich and thereafter immediately went to Norderney, where he became a substitute pastor.[13]

10. Document by Carl Siegert to the Gestapo-Osnabrück of December 22, 1938, Landeskirchliches Archiv Hannover, N 147, Entschädigungssache Paul Leo. "St. John/Crabapple: 100 years St. John" (Fredericksburg 1997), 115.

11. Archiv der Philipps-Universität Marburg, Bestand 305 a Nr. 8452, *Akademische Vereinigung*, Laufzeit 1912–35.

12. *Osnabrücker Tageblatt* (October 20, 1930).

13. *Kirchliches Amtsblatt der ev.-luth Landeskirche Hannovers* 1927, 58; document by Carl Siegert to the Gestapo-Osnabrück of December 22, 1938, Landeskirchliches Archiv Hannover, N 147, Entschädigungssache Paul Leo, n9; and *Osnabrücker Tageblatt* (October 20, 1930).

First Positions as Pastor from 1922–29

In the waning years of the German Empire, two German islands in the North Sea developed a distinctive profile in relation to Jewish vacationers. Borkum was considered inimical to Jews, while Norderney was considered friendly to them.[14] Not by pure accident, the *Landeskirchenamt* delegated Paul Leo to serve as the substitute pastor at Norderney.

The years between the Great Wars (1919–39) was the final period for the church to exercise the nineteenth-century approach to pastoral service, namely, to care for a growing number of the faithful by increasing the number of pastorates in a congregation and thereby avoiding the expensive construction of new church buildings. For the last time in 1926, an additional pastorate was announced for the three Lutheran congregations of Osnabrück, specifically a sixth pastor at St. Mary.[15] From Norderney, Paul Leo applied for this sixth position at St. Mary. Richard Karwehl, a friend of Leo, who occupied the fifth position, probably had alerted him to this.[16]

As pastor, Richard Karwehl was also a member of the church council at St. Mary, which was responsible for calling the new pastor. He may have exercised influence so that Paul Leo was included on the list of three names, which had been agreed upon in a pre-election by the church council.[17] In the election by the congregation following this, however, another applicant, Hans Rapp, received the most votes.[18] Richard Karwehl subsequently complained in a letter to his mother that these "Philistines" had

14. Cf. Pauluhn, *Zur Geschichte der Juden auf Norderney*; and Andryszak and Bramkamp, *Jüdisches Leben auf Norderney*.

15. The concept of dividing congregations by adding new pastorates was continued for a few decades and had its high point in the 1960s. Since the 1990s, the number of pastorates has been reduced and congregations are being joined together.

16. Brandy, "Gustav Oehlert und Paul Leo," 398.

17. Brandy, "Gustav Oehlert und Paul Leo," 398n15.

18. Hans Rapp (born 1897) served from 1925–26 as substitute pastor at St. Mary, 1926–39, in the sixth position at St. Mary, and from 1939–60 in the second position at St. Paul's, Osnabrück.

not elected Leo, since he was "a 7/8 Jew."[19] Even if this testimony from a direct witness has high probability, one must add that due to the cost, this position had been staffed from 1925–26 by a substitute pastor, namely Hans Rapp. The congregation in 1926 had simply decided in favor of the already known pastor, who in some ways became his own successor.

After his time as substitute pastor, Paul Leo finally received a permanent position in 1927 and was transferred from Norderney at the far north of the regional church to its southern border. His new congregation was in Neuhaus, deep in the Solling Mountains.[20] Paul Leo's immediate predecessor there was Hermann Karwehl, the younger brother of Richard Karwehl. One may assume there was a certain network in action. Perhaps Paul Leo was informed by his friend, Richard Karwehl, of the position that was becoming vacant, placing himself into consideration or having been suggested by Karwehl. In any case, Paul Leo got to know the state district president in the Solling Mountains region, Paul Siegert, and his daughter, Anna Siegert, whom he married a few years later.[21]

In the 1920s, Paul Leo continued his systematic investigation and study of church doctrine. Already after his first theological exam in 1919, he designated a theme for his dissertation for which he received the Lic. theol, the licentiate in theology from the University of Marburg.[22] This title is equivalent to the later Dr. theol., the Doctor of Theology.

His dissertation topic was "The Effect of Basil the Great on the Monasticism of His Time." Prior to Basil, "an individualistic ascetic ideal" dominated the community of monks.[23] With Basil

19. Quoted in Brandy, "Gustav Oehlert und Paul Leo," 398n15.

20. "24.4.1927 P. Lic. Theol. P. F. Leo in Neuhaus-Silberborn, bisher auf Norderney," in *Kirchliches Amtsblatt der ev.-luth. Landeskirche Hannovers*, 1927, 58. Cf. Meyer, *Die Pastoren*, 2:186. *Osnabrücker Tageblatt* (October 20, 1930).

21. Document by Carl Siegert to the Gestapo-Osnabrück of December 22, 1938, Landeskirchliches Archiv Hannover, N 147, Entschädigungssache Paul Leo, n9.

22. *Osnabrücker Tageblatt* (October 20, 1930).

23. Leo, "Die Wirkung Basilius' des Grossen," (1929) 4.

then came the "evangelical-biblical change of the ascetic ideals."[24] It was only through the intensive study of the Bible that monasticism obtained its "intellectual foundation and justification."[25] Basil's success was conditioned by the central role played by doctrinal discussions among the monks.[26] Paul Leo's conclusion concerning his protagonist could also be seen as the conclusion for his own life: "The drive to overcome the world has been victorious over the pure flight from the world."[27]

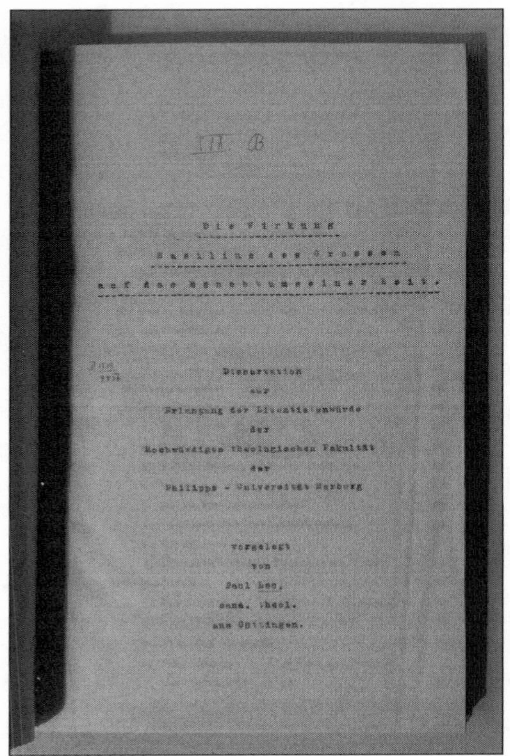

Die Wirkung

Basilius des Grossen

auf das Mönchtum seiner Zeit.

Dissertation

zur

Erlangung der Licentiatenwürde

der

Hochwürdigen theologischen Fakultät

der

Philipps - Universität Marburg

vorgelegt

von

Paul Leo,

cand. theol.

aus Göttingen.

Title Page from Dissertation

24. Leo, "Die Wirkung Basilius' des Grossen," (1929) 3n22.
25. Leo, "Die Wirkung Basilius' des Grossen," (1929) 4n22.
26. Leo, "Die Wirkung Basilius' des Grossen," (1929) 3–4n22.
27. Leo, "Die Wirkung Basilius' des Grossen," (1928) 142.

In the 1920s, Paul Leo enjoyed interacting with others and was interested in theological discussions. In the fall of 1926, twelve younger pastors of the church met for discussions that they called the Deinser Conference.[28] Paul Leo was its cofounder.[29] The meetings of the conference focused especially on the topics of "youth" and "dialectical theology."[30] On November 13, 1929, Paul Leo presented a paper on "Confessional Church and People's Church."[31] For a time he belonged to the steering committee of the conference.[32]

This conference was an indication that the younger generation of pastors wanted to create its own space parallel to the official structures of the church. This was by no means new to the church. A common example is the *Protestantenverein* (Protestant Union) of the 1860s to 1890s, which formulated ever new ideas concerning the modernization of the Protestant church and which existed for several generations of pastors.[33] At the beginning of the twentieth century, these younger pastors joined together and founded, according to the same intentions, their own groups, such the *Verband der Freunde der evangelischen Wahrheit* (Association of the Friends of the Protestant Truth).[34]

In the literature concerning the *Deinser Jungevangelische Konferenz*, the idealistic approach of this conference has been emphasized, but much less the aspect of its network. Accordingly, for example, the Osnabrück pastor, Richard Karwehl, in a paper from June 1931 on "Political Messianism" pointed already

28. Brunotte, "Die jungevangelische Bewegung," 206.

29. This conference was later renamed Hannoversche Konferenz jüngerer Theologen and in 1929 finally as Hannoversche Jungevangelische Konferenz. Cf. Brandy, "Gustav Oehlert und Paul Leo," 389n15. Klügel, *Die lutherische Landeskirche*, 12.

30. Brandy, "Gustav Oehlert und Paul Leo," 389n15.

31. Brandy, "Gustav Oehlert und Paul Leo," 389n15. Brunotte, "Die jungevangelische Bewegung," 180n27.

32. Brunotte, "Die jungevangelische Bewegung," 19n27.

33. Rädisch, *Die Evangelisch-lutherische Landeskirche*, 192–205. Rolffs, *Evangelische Kirchenkunde Niedersachsens*, 214.

34. Hübinger, *Kulturprotestantismus und Politik*, 68.

in a clear-sighted manner to "the critical points in national socialism."[35] More importantly, however, it seems these were "active theologians of the postwar generation" who met occasionally for discussions.[36] The need of a younger generation of pastors simply to maintain collegial and human contacts with each other was most likely the essence of these conferences. Not by accident, two colleagues whom Paul Leo got to know there, Richard Karwehl and Otto Piper,[37] proved to be helpful to him in his later life. During that time Richard Karwehl supported Paul Leo's application for the sixth position at St. Mary and probably later his transfer to Osnabrück. During his immigration to the USA, Otto Piper secured for him a position as guest professor.[38]

Another example of Paul Leo's engagement in the 1920s involves his participation in the "World Conference of Faith and Order" at Lausanne in 1927.[39] The concern of the younger pastors there was to think the faith anew and to avoid it sliding into a religion of law, or conversely into magic and mysticism.[40] This continued in April 1929 among a smaller circle in which Paul

35. Klügel, *Die lutherische Landeskirche*, 12n28. The presentation was entitled "Nationalsozialismus und Kirche." Karwehl presented this paper in a meeting of the *Jungevangelische Konferenz* (Conference of Young Protestants), June 10–11, 1931. The lecture was shortly thereafter published in a journal: "Richard Karwehl, Politisches Messiastum. Zur Auseinandersetzung von Kirche und Nationalsozialismus," *Zwischen den Zeiten* 9 (1931) 519–43. Reprint: "Richard Karwehl, Politisches Messiastum. Zur Auseinandersetzung von Kirche und Nationalsozialismus," in Fürst, "Dialektische Theologie," in *Scheidung und Bewährung*, 19–41. Cf. Brunotte, "Die jungevangelische Bewegung," 190n27. Becker, *Zur Rolle des Osnabrücker*, 19. Perels took June 30, 1931, as the date of the lecture. Cf. Perels, "Richard Karwehl," 166.

36. Klügel, *Die lutherische Landeskirche*, 12n28.

37. At that time Otto Piper was private lecturer (*Privatdozent*) and since 1930 Professor of Theology at Münster. Cf. Brandy, "Gustav Oehlert und Paul Leo," 389n15.

38. Eva Leo, "Biographie Paul Leos," Unpublished Manuscript (Dubuque 1960), in Landeskirchliches Archiv Hannover, S1 HII 920. Nachlass Prof. Lic. Paul Leo, Dubuque (Iowa), Bl. 39–54.

39. Brandy, "Gustav Oehlert und Paul Leo," 389n15.

40. Wolfes, *Protestantische Theologie*, 304–5.

Leo again participated.[41] Here, too, one may add that the international networking of Protestant pastors had been going on for several decades and this always especially interested the younger pastors.[42] After his unsuccessful application for the newly created sixth pastorate at St. Mary in 1926, Paul Leo finally obtained a position in Osnabrück in 1930.

Pastor in Osnabrück, 1930–38

The position in Osnabrück resulted from a larger development in the church and therefore needs to be explained. For a long time, a Lutheran pastor had overseen everything in the congregation. However, in the nineteenth century innovations were introduced, to which also belonged special pastors, confirmed by the new church constitution after World War I.[43] These entailed approximately thirty pastors who officially had a preaching position in a congregation, while they were delegated to a church district; each one received from the respective superintendent a plethora of individual tasks.

41. This meeting took place with the title *Ausschuß für Glaube und Kirchenverfassung* (Committee for Faith and Order) in Waldenburg and was organized by Friedrich Siegmund-Schultze, who himself had to emigrate in 1933 because he had been helping Jews to emigrate. Cf. Brandy, "Gustav Oehlert und Paul Leo," 389n15.

42. For example, Weltkongress für freies Christentum und religiösen Fortschritt (World Congress for Liberal Christianity and Religious Progress) held in Berlin 1910 and Paris 1913.

43. "Sonderseelsorger" (special counselor) is the present-day designation. According to the Constitution of the Church of Hanover from 1922, one called them in the 1920s and 1930s "Landesgeistliche" (area pastors) and "Anstaltsgeistliche" (pastors for institutions) and together as "Geistliche mit besonderem Auftrag" (pastors with a special charge). Cf. Meyer, *Die Pastoren*, 2:237n19. Blitz, *Evangelisch-lutherisches Gemeindebuch*, 28. As of December 31, 1930, nine area pastors and twenty-two pastors for institutions were active in the church at large. Cf. Rolffs, *Evangelische Kirchenkunde Niedersachsens*, 57. From 1924–39 one area pastor was delegated to the church district of Osnabrück and from 1929–38 Paul Leo as pastor for institutions.

The first special counselor, Paul Neumann,[44] who in 1930 had been delegated to the church district of Osnabrück, was entrusted with a considerable number of tasks.[45] The nature of these tasks is significant. Because some tasks did not meet with favor by the Osnabrück pastors, these tasks were consequently bound together by the superintendent in the first special counseling position. This can be seen very clearly in the example of counseling at the institution for the mentally disabled.[46] In the 1920s, one of the pastors at St. Mary conducted a church service in the chapel of the institution for the mentally disabled every other week. For several years Hans Bodensieck was responsible for this.[47] He had arranged with the respective Roman Catholic priest, who was responsible for the services the other weeks, that this pastor would conduct almost all the Sunday services. This arrangement only came into the open after a complaint.

Paul Neumann developed the *Evangelische Wohlfahrtsdienst* (Protestant Welfare) as the local agency for diaconal work. These activities were financed by the congregational treasuries of St.

44. Paul Neumann (1888–1979) was the first special counselor of the church district of Osnabrück from May 1, 1930–39/45. Cf. Landeskirchliches Archiv Hannover, B7 Nr. 666, Personalakte Neumann, Bl. 15.

45. The roughly two dozen individual tasks were, among others: Business Executive of the Protestant Welfare Service of Osnabrück, Head of the Children's Library, Head of the Mission at the Railway Station (including the kitchen for the homeless), Counselor at the Children's Home at Schölerberg, and District Youth Pastor. Cf. minutes of the district church assemblies since 1927 and the annual reports of the Welfare Service of the District Church Archive of Osnabrück.

46. In the correspondence of that time, the designation *Irrenanstalt* (Institution of the Mentally Retarded) and *Irrenhaus* (Home for the Mentally Retarded) was used consistently and therefore we continue to use it here. It is the still existing institution on the Osnabrück hill of St. Gertrude, which, from 1868–1900 was called Hannoversche Provinzialständige Irrenanstalt (Institution for the Mentally Retarded of the Province of Hanover). The exact location of the church service was at St. Gertrude, Senator-Wagner-Weg 8 (present day address).

47. Hans Bodensieck (1881–1953) was pastor at St. Mary in Osnabrück (1907–50). Cf. Landeskirchliches Archiv Hannover, B7 Nr. 454, Personalakte Hans Bodensieck.

Mary, St. Catherine, the Luther Congregation, and the Osnabrück Evangelical-Reformed congregation.[48]

Presumably because of the Osnabrück superintendent, Ernst Rolffs, who had good relations to the *Landeskirchenamt*[49] and was highly regarded as a church historian (regularly connected with the *Landeskirchenamt* as examiner in the second theological exam of the vicars), the church district of Osnabrück in 1930 also obtained a second special counseling position.

While the salary of the first special counselor was paid from the treasury of the *Landeskirchenamt*, by contrast, for the second position it was expected that the salary would be financed by the treasury of the church district. Because the church district and not the *Landeskirchenamt* was to guarantee the salary of this second special counselor, unlike the first special counseling position, the voice of Osnabrück became relevant for staffing the position. Ernst Rolffs as superintendent had the most influence in staffing the position. Paul Leo was selected, and one may assume either that Richard Karwehl had interceded for him or that Leo had become known in Osnabrück on account of his application for the sixth position at St. Mary a few years earlier.[50]

The formal process for Paul Leo's appointment to this office went as follows: The *Landeskirchenamt* and the board of the church district agreed in April 1930 on Paul Leo.[51] The *Landeskirchenamt* informed him in June 1930, first informally, of his impending

48. Cf. Broschüre Fünfter Kreiskirchentag, 26. The fourth congregational district of St. Catherine had become independent in 1926 as "Luther Congregation," but was still economically united with St. Catherine as an "Association." Cf. Vermögensverwaltung des Gesamtverbandes, Niedersächsische Staatsarchive, Außenstelle Osnabrück, Rep. 430 Dez. 400 Nr. 1693.

49. Ernst Rolffs (1867–1947): 1892–95 at the Preachers' Seminary Erichsburg, 1902–38 pastor at St. Catherine, and 1921–August 30, 1938, simultaneously superintendent of the church district of Osnabrück.

50. It was certainly not a disadvantage that twenty years earlier than Leo, Ernst Rolffs had attended the Preachers' Seminary Erichsburg.

51. Cf. decision of the executive committee of the church district of Osnabrück from April 1, 1930, Archiv des Kirchenkreises Osnabrück, Personalakte Pastor Leo.

nomination for the special counseling position in Osnabrück,[52] and shortly thereafter told him of his official appointment effective October 1, 1930.[53] Induction to his responsibilities took place on October 18, 1930, in the sacristy of St. Catherine[54] with his installation on October 19, 1930, at a church service.[55] At the same time, Ernst Rolffs designated tasks for Paul Leo.[56] The criterion for the list of responsibilities was that the part-time positions needed to contribute concretely to the financing of the second special counseling position, so that the treasury of the church district was not burdened by the salary of Paul Leo. These included:

1. Institution of healing and care
2. Teaching institution for midwifery
3. Institution for teaching those with impaired speech and hearing
4. City home for care
5. City Hospital
6. Hospital of St. Mary
7. Court prisons

For instance, counseling in the institution for teaching those with impaired speech and hearing[57] was income from payment by the supporting institution, the province of Hanover, and could be used for Paul Leo's teaching religious instruction and the confirmation class. The same was true for Leo's activity in the teaching institution for midwifery.[58] Here the fees for baptiz-

52. Communication of Paul Leo to Ernst Rolffs from June 27, 1930, Archiv des Kirchenkreises Osnabrück, Personalakte Pastor Leo.

53. *Osnabrück Tageblatt* (October 20, 1930).

54. Minutes of the induction of Leo, October 18, 1930, Archiv des Kirchenkreises Osnabrück, Personalakte Pastor Leo.

55. *Osnabrück Tageblatt* (October 20, 1930).

56. Letter of Ernst Rolffs to Paul Leo from October 2, 1930, Archiv des Kirchenkreises Osnabrück, Personalakte Pastor Leo.

57. Present terminology: *Gehörlosenseelsorge* (Counseling of the Hearing Impaired).

58. The sponsorship of the teaching institution for midwifery was

ing infants were a solid source of income for the treasury of the church district.[59] Leo's activity in the City Hospital also generated income, which was used to pay Paul Leo for teaching religious instruction to the nursing students.

Establishing the first special counseling position was regarded with favor by the Osnabrück pastors, because the assigned tasks were bundled together without any special payment for the pastor. For Paul Leo's position, the paid tasks that were tied together as portions of his salary had been sought out by the pastors in the financially difficult 1920s. The issue of responsibility for these tasks had for years led to quarrels among the pastors and only shortly after Leo assumed his office had this been settled "from above."[60]

Soon after his transfer to Osnabrück, private disaster struck Paul Leo. Anna Leo, his wife, died within a few days after the birth of their daughter Anna due to puerperal fever.[61] Leo himself also became sick for some time and later for a yet longer period. Several times he was unable to work; in the summer of 1932 he was absent because of medical treatment.[62] Though the *Landeskirchenamt* had declined to pay child subsidy for Paul Leo's daughter in the beginning of 1932,[63] the medical treatment in the summer of 1932 was

transferred in 1937 from the Province of Hanover to the City of Osnabrück and the Women's Hospital was joined with the City Hospital. Cf. Drewes, "Geschichte der öffentlichen Krankenhäuser," 10.

59. In the 1920s and 1930s, approximately 20 percent the children in Osnabrück were born out of wedlock. Because these baptisms were not done at St. Mary, this was a steady source of income.

60. Cf. "Urteil des Landeskirchengerichts in Hannover in der Sitzung vom 14.11.1930," Landeskirchliches Archiv Hannover; Akten der ehemaligen Generalsuperintendentur Aurich, Akte "Die schweren Kämpfe zwischen den Geistlichen in Osnabrück 1927–1930." The Depositum, which was consulted, is now divided into the Deposita L5f Nr. 285 and L5f Nr. 286.

61. Cf. the handwritten CV of Paul Leo from October 19, 1930, Archiv des Kirchenkreises Osnabrück, Personalakte Paul Leo.

62. Paul Leo asked several times for extensions during his medical treatment. Cf. the exchange of letters between Paul Leo and Ernst Rolffs during the summer of 1932. Archiv des Kirchenkreises Osnabrück, Personalakte Paul Leo.

63. Letter of the *Landeskirchenamt* Hanover to Ernst Rolffs from February

paid.[64] Finally in the summer of 1932, Ernst Rolffs placed gentle pressure on Leo to resume his activity as soon as possible.[65] Since he began his position, Paul Leo had received a salary without corresponding performance of work. Therefore, Ernst Rolffs unsuccessfully sought from his superior, Superintendent General Wilhelm Schomerus,[66] the transfer of Paul Leo.[67] Beginning in fall 1932, Paul Leo was again active as a pastor in Osnabrück.

Structural changes to the Lutheran church in Osnabrück the following year had major consequences for Paul Leo. All Lutheran pastors in Osnabrück were strongly opposed by the state and the Nazis from 1933 to 1945. As an example, I will mention one of the pastors of St. Mary, Friedrich Grussendorf.[68] Already in 1919–32, Grussendorf encountered events like the following: "In a large gathering in the Festive Hall related to World War I, the accusation was made that pastors were murderers, who had encouraged the people to persevere during the war."[69] Similar experiences were endured by all Osnabrück pastors each day in the postwar period. Only in a limited way, therefore, was the anti-church orientation of the succeeding National Socialist movement (the Nazis called themselves National Socialists) really a new experience.

As for Grußendorf in particular, on Sundays beginning in 1933 in front of his church in Osnabrück-Eversburg, SA-men

---

17, 1932, Archiv des Kirchenkreises Osnabrück, Personalakte Paul Leo.

64. Letter of Ernst Rolffs to the *Landeskirchenamt* Hanover from August 8, 1932, Archiv des Kirchenkreises Osnabrück, Personalakte Paul Leo.

65. Letter of Ernst Rolffs to Paul Leo from August 2, 1932, Archiv des Kirchenkreises Osnabrück, Personalakte Paul Leo. In this letter Ernst Rolffs tells Paul Leo that due to overwork, Leo's colleagues are hardly able to substitute for him.

66. Wilhelm Schomerus (1864–1943), Superintendent General in Aurich from 1925–33.

67. Letter of Wilhelm Schomerus to Ernst Rolffs from July 8, 1932, Archiv des Kirchenkreises Osnabrück, Personalakte Paul Leo.

68. Friedrich Grußendorf (1871–1958) was pastor at St. Mary in Osnabrück (1906–39).

69. *Kirchenbote* (Church Messenger) from July 1937. The "Kirchenbote der evang.-lutherischen Gemeinden Osnabrücks" was the bulletin of all Osnabrück Lutheran congregations from April 1, 1919, to June 1941.

(*Sturmabteilung*, that is, the battle organization of the Nazi party) met in working clothes and made threats from outside the church services with calls such as, "Come out here you pig, we want to cut off your head!"[70] He tolerated such things, even though the number of those who were attending Sunday morning church services declined to 10 percent between 1933 and 1938.[71] His principle was to provoke but subtly, for example, "He once preached about 'the thousand years' time' to the sick in the hospitals. At the beginning of his devotion, he raised up in front of them two books, the Bible and *Mein Kampf*. 'From which should I read?' he asked. The answer was so clear that the party and the *Gestapo* (*Geheime Staatspolizei*, the secret state police with virtually unlimited authority) raged in anger. But nothing happened to the pastor."[72]

Sometimes Grussendorf also openly declared where he stood. "The reporter himself witnessed one and a half decades ago that Fritz Grussendorf debated with SA-men and at the end he called out to them: 'When nobody will talk anymore about your Hitler, Christ will still be known!' One did not dare to touch him."[73] Actually, he was once put into custody by the Osnabrück *Gestapo*, but after three days he was released again because unrest arose among the common members of his congregation.[74]

Beyond the everyday animosity, there was also a regulated *Gleichschaltung* ("forced cooptation") of the local church. For practical purposes, regular church members would leave, and totally different personnel appeared who were striving to control the functions of the church. This can be illustrated by an incident at the Luther Congregation. A church council election was scheduled for May 14, 1933. The local group leader of the NSDAP (National Socialist

70. Communication of February 7, 2005, by Karl-Heinz Schorege, who was a confirmand of Grussendorf in 1936.

71. Cf. Meyer, *Chronik der Kirchengemeinde*, in Archiv der Kirchengemeinde St. Michaelis, Osnabrück.

72. *Freie Presse* (April 8, 1953). The *Freie Prese* was a daily newspaper in Osnabrück that ceased circulation in the 1960s.

73. *Freie Presse* (April 8, 1953).

74. Lindemann, "Fritz Grussendorf," in *Von Assmann bis Wöberking*, 32–34.

German Workers' Party, that is, the Nazi party) informed Pastor Wilhelm Saalbach a few days earlier about his candidates:[75] "In the following we announce our candidates . . . any opposing candidacy appears to be useless and would only cause utmost unrest and revolt in the congregation."[76] The day before the election, this local group leader told the NSDAP and SA members in his local group who should be elected; and so they were.[77] The pastor subsequently asked for a conversation. He and several of the new council members met in the apartment of the local group leader of the NSDAP to talk, and a quarrel erupted. The newly elected first candidate of the NSDAP list,[78] a member of the district leadership in the NSDAP, finally threatened Wilhelm Saalbach with a beating and the pastor countered with the words, "then just hit me."[79]

Similar events also could be reported for the other two Lutheran congregations of Osnabrück. The forced cooptation of the congregations tapered off within a few years, because the NSDAP became openly antagonistic to the church and the Nazi church council members no longer attended the meetings.[80]

Concerning the forced cooptation of the church district, the following is noteworthy. In 1925 an annual church rally was first started, the "*Kreiskirchentag*" (Church District Assembly). After 1933 there was no longer any discussion time held at the assembly. Whereas for the first seven annual assemblies extended minutes

75. Wilhelm Saalbach (1891–1962) was pastor at the Luther Congregation, Osnabrück (1927–60), Landeskirchliches Archiv Hannover, B7 Nr. 1040 Personalakte Wilhelm Saalbach.

76. Letter of Rudolf Arnoldi to Wilhelm Saalbach from May 5, 1933, Archiv des Kirchenkreises Osnabrück, Akte St. Katharinenkirche Osnabrück.

77. Communication of Saalbach to Ernst Rolffs from May 20, 1933, Archiv des Kirchenkreises Osnabrück, Akte St. Katharinenkirche Osnabrück.

78. Communication of Saalbach to Ernst Rolffs from May 20, 1933, Archiv des Kirchenkreises Osnabrück, Akte St. Katharinenkirche Osnabrück.

79. Reconstructed minutes of the meeting from May 10, 1933, Archiv des Kirchenkreises Osnabrück, Akte St. Katharinenkirche Osnabrück.

80. Letter of Ernst Rolffs to the Landeskirchenamt Hannover from February 16, 1938, Archiv des Kirchenkreises Osnabrück, Akte Kirchenvorstand zu St. Katharinenkirche Osnabrück.

have been preserved, the minutes of the eighth meeting in the summer of 1933 consists only of one page. Concerning the election of the steering committee of the church district we read: "Then one proceeds to the election of the steering committee of the church district. Mr. Münzer suggests the following members. . . . Since no contrary proposals are made, the election is by acclamation. The elected members accept the election."[81] All thirteen Lutheran pastors of Osnabrück were present, including Paul Leo.[82] Why the otherwise quarrelsome Osnabrück pastors here agreed to an election by acclamation is beside the point. Wilhelm Münzer, who for the first time appears as the leader, two years later gave the decisive anti-Jewish speech against Paul Leo.[83] Another church district assembly was not convened until 1945.

Since the *Machtergreifung* (seizing of power by the Nazis) in the beginning of 1933, interference by the state and the Nazis in the affairs of the church increased. Consequently, the Confessing Church was founded in Germany with its seminal document, the *Barmen Declaration* of 1934. In the church of Hanover, a *Bekenntnisgemeinschaft* (confessional community) then was formed.

The Osnabrück members of this confessional community, all six pastors of St. Mary plus Paul Leo, called themselves the Osnabrück Circle. The Osnabrück Circle came under continual suspicion, due to its supposed affinity to the state, by the *Landeskirchenamt* and the *Bruderrat* (Council of Brethren), as the governing board of the Confessing community in Hanover was called. For all practical purposes, its effectiveness ended

81. Minutes of the District Church Assembly from August 3, 1933, Archiv des Kirchenkreises Osnabrück, Akte 7. Kreiskirchentag.

82. Minutes of the District Church Assembly from August 3, 1933, Archiv des Kirchenkreises Osnabrück, Akte 7. Kreiskirchentag.

83. Münzer was an employee (cf. Gartmann and Reichel, "Aufstieg und Machtübernahme," 176–77), who was active in rightist splinter groups since 1924 (cf. Junk and Sellmeyer, *Stationen auf dem Weg*, 251), local group leader from 1932–34, and district leader of the NSDAP Osnabrück from 1934–40. In 1933 he became a member of the city council (cf. Rademacher, *Wer war wer im Gau Weser-Ems*, 126–31) and on November 9, 1936, he left the Lutheran church (cf. Archiv des Kirchenkreises Osnabrück, Akte Austrittsbewegung).

by its demonstrative exodus from the Confessing community in December 1935.[84] With regard to the state and the NSDAP, the Osnabrück Confessing pastors were compliant. Due to their restraint, they protected themselves and survived the Nazi time relatively unharmed, except for Paul Leo."

Compared to the 1920s, which was characterized by extreme quarrels among all the Lutheran pastors of Osnabrück, after 1933 they maintained a kind of truce.[85] This was expressed in the joint composition of a confession. On April 27, 1933, eleven of the thirteen Lutheran pastors of Osnabrück, among them Paul Leo, met in the sacristy of St. Catherine to discuss and decide on a text,[86] which they handed out to some external colleagues under the title *Osnabrücker Bekenntnis* (Osnabrück Confession).[87] It did not, however, become known "far beyond the area of its composers and signers"[88] and was drowned out by the "voluminous production of confessions" in 1933.[89]

The Osnabrück Confession had adopted largely the contents of the Altona Confession from January 11, 1933, which had

84. Document Bornschein, Loewenfeld, Bodensieck, Leo, Karwehl, Thimme of December 12, 1935, Landeskirchliches Archiv Hannover, S1 HI 204, Bl. 64.

85. The title of the hand file of the Superintendent General Wilhelm Schomerus is telling: "Die schweren Kämpfe zwischen den Geistlichen in Osnabrück 1927–1930"("The Severe Conflicts between the Pastors in Osnabrück 1927–1930") n59.

86. "Das 'Osnabrücker Bekenntnis' vom 27.4.1933," in Klügel, *Die lutherische Landeskirche*, 21–22n8. The date of the meeting comes from a document by Wilhelm Schomerus of May 9, 1933, Landeskirchliches Archiv Hannover, S1 HI 204, Bl. 17.

87. Cf. Johannes Bornschein's accompanying letter to the Osnabrück Confession of May 4, 1933, Landeskirchliches Archiv Hannover, S1 HI 204, Bl. 16–17.

88. Klügel, *Die lutherische Landeskirche*, 51n28. While the Osnabrück Confession of April 27, 1933, received little attention during the Nazi time, later it was interpreted in different ways. For example, Perels, "Richard Karwehl," 169; Becker, *Zur Rolle des Osnabrücker*, 24–25n34; Simon, "Richard Karwehl," 186; Glufke, "Richard Karwehl," 176–78; Reese, *Bekenntnis und Bekennen*, 156; and Klügel, *Die lutherische Landeskirche*, 51–52n28.

89. Reese, *Bekenntnis und Bekennen*, 11n87.

been published a few months earlier and which took a stance on public events.[90]

In contrast to the Altona Confession, the Osnabrück Confession expressly mentioned the Old Testament, perhaps because Paul Leo was its coauthor.[91] At the same time, one notices that the condition of the Jews was not thematized in the Osnabrück Confession of Spring 1933.[92] However, the topic of the Jews gained in significance after 1933 and pertained concretely to Paul Leo.

Around April 1, 1933, the first anti-Jewish wave initiated by the Nazis swept through the German Reich. On this occasion, the Hanover Bishop August Marahrens invited Paul Leo as a Lutheran pastor of the church for a discussion on May 6, 1933.[93] What was intended as a private discussion ended with the charge for Paul Leo to put his thoughts in writing. As a theologian with a doctorate and as a pastor who was very interested in the affairs of the church, Paul Leo did not hesitate to send to Bishop Marahrens an elaborate treatise.

Paul Leo expressed himself in the memorandum, "Church and Judaism," largely in view of the public events.[94] He stated that

90. Brandy, "Gustav Oehlert und Paul Leo," 398–99n15.

91. "The task of the church is to sharpen the conscience and to proclaim the gospel according to the rule of the Old and New Testament in line with the confession of our fathers." Osnabrück Confession, in Klügel, *Die lutherische Landeskirche*, 21n8.

92. Smid explicitly noted for the first time that the reference to Judaism was missing in the Osnabrück Confession. Cf. Reese, *Bekenntnis und Bekennen*, 176–78n87. The reason was that the authors of the Osnabrück Confession were concerned about the question of the place of the church in the state, as Smid confirmed with further perspectives: "The responsible theologians and church people in spring of 1933 were not really concerned . . . about the state's treatment of the Jews and also not about the problem of 'the church and the Jewish question.' Its agenda is primarily to fathom the relationship of the church with the new state." Smid, *Deutscher Protestantismus und Judentum*, 480n87.

93. Rocker, "Der Umgang der Landeskirche Hannovers," 33.

94. Leo, "Denkschrift," 189–96n8. In the explanation we find anti-Semitic tones: "Pastor Paul Leo . . . also expresses anti-Semitic sentiments in his 1933 memorandum on 'Church and Judaism.' . . . Leo's memorandum maintains that Germany had suffered from the Jews." Cf. Werner Cohn, "Bearers of

a segment of the German population continuously rejected the assimilation of the Jews and that a segment of the Jews did not want to be assimilated, as one sees with Zionism. It was wrong to pass over the situation of the Jews in silence: "Among the German citizenry, the attitude of an educated and benevolent person was to be silent concerning the issue of the Jews."[95] The present situation is the product of this mistaken historical development. Leo found one possible way to deal with this situation in the Bible: "Decisive for us are the words of Paul: 'Let every person be subject to the governing authorities.' . . . We do not owe obedience to our governing authority because we approve its measures but because it is instituted for us by God."[96] Concretely this meant for a Jew in Germany: "If we remained within the German state, we are subjects of the German authorities and owe them obedience."[97] Pointedly, Paul Leo wrote concerning the baptized Jews: "If we ask about the position of the baptized Jew in the church, then any ethnic point of view has to be silenced. For the church there is no German or Jewish ethnicity. There is neither Jew nor Greek."[98]

Paul Leo sharpened this later thought and in relation to the "Union of Non-Aryan Christians" advocated the founding of separate "Jewish-Christian" congregations.[99] To that effect, he published papers and conducted lectures from 1935 to 1937.[100]

Common Fate?," 327–66.

95. Leo, "Denkschrift," 189.

96. Leo, 189–96n8.

97. Leo, 189–96n8.

98. Leo, 189–96n8.

99. Founding name: "Reichsverband christlich-deutscher Staatsbürger nichtarischer oder nicht rein arischer Abstammung e.V." The Association existed from July 20, 1933 to August 11, 1939. It changed its name several times. "It seems to have been interested only in pastors who themselves were involved, namely Gurland, Benfey, or Paul Leo." Hans Otte, Mitteilungen aus dem Landeskirchlichen Archiv Hannover 5 (October 2006), 17.

100. For example, the article "Der Nichtarier als Christ," *Mitteilungsblatt des Reichsverbandes der nichtarischen Christen* 10 (1935) and the lecture "Die nichtarischen Christen und die Kirche" presented in Frankfurt on November 10, 1937, Landeskirchliche Archiv Hannover, S1 HII 920 Nachlass Prof. Lic. Paul Leo, Dubuque (Iowa), Bl. 72–82.

He now emphasized more strongly the break from ethnic Judaism through baptism: "For all of us, the religious and ethnic ties to Judaism already were dissolved through baptism."[101]

For the Osnabrück colleagues in the Nazi time, Paul Leo was considered an expert on the Old Testament, while actually he was one on the New Testament.[102] The *Landeskirchenamt* in 1936 made the pastors attend a joint convention, since there was a split among the pastors into German Christians and Confessing Church pastors. At the first Osnabrück convention on April 28, 1937, Paul Leo presented the main paper with the title "The Theological Exegesis of the Old Testament."[103] He started with Luke 24:27: "Then beginning with Moses and all the prophets, [Jesus] interpreted to them the things about himself in all the scriptures." According to Leo, the triune God speaks in the Old Testament and therefore this is a witness to Christ and contains Christ in a veiled form.

When the exclusion of and lawlessness against the Jews by the state occurred after 1933,[104] Paul Leo was gradually relieved of his different part-time responsibilities since they were connected with the state. At first, he lost his responsibility for the prisons. This was to be expected, because the prisons were under the authority of the Prussian province of Hanover, which meant they were directly state institutions. Ernst Rolffs wrote at that time to his superior Wilhelm Schomerus: "With the Aryan paragraph in the new law for civil servants, pastor Lic. Leo will be affected, since on his father's and his mother's side he descends from Jewish families. And insofar as

101. Thus, Paul Leo in 1935. Here is a translation: "For all of us, the religious and ethnic [*volksmässige*] ties to Judaism have been broken precisely by this baptism . . . we state with emphasis that we who are baptized non-Aryans, whether of mixed or unmixed blood, continue to consider ourselves as Germans." *Mitteilungsblatt des Reichsverbandes christlich-deutscher Staatsbürger nichtarischer oder nicht rein arischer Abstammung e.V.*, October 1935, 55, as quoted from Cohn, "Bearers of Common Fate?," 327–66n93.

102. Letter of Ernst Rolffs to all Osnabrück pastors from April 7, 1937, Archiv des Kirchenkreises Osnabrück, Akte Konvent.

103. Copy in the Archiv des Kirchenkreises Osnabrück, Akte Konvent.

104. The basis was the "Durchführungsverordnung zur Wiederherstellung des Berufsbeamtentums" (Implementing Regulation to Reinstitute the Profession of Civil Servants), effective May 4, 1933.

he is a counselor for the provincial institution of healing and care, the prison, and the institution for the hearing and speech impaired, he is in the service of the Provincial Administration, that is, of Justice."[105] What was expected did occur only a few months later. In the middle of August came the instruction by the state administration of the prisons that the discharge of Paul Leo would follow. Therefore, the *Landeskirchenamt* decided that Paul Leo himself should give them notice.[106] For the *Landeskirchenamt* and the superintendent there was the practical concern that the state contract for counseling in prisons be discontinued by the church. Paul Leo then was discharged by the state on October 1, 1933.[107]

In the two years following, he lost all his part-time positions. In the literature one reads how the legal domination by the Nazis in 1933 was met on the Lutherans side with goodwill and a kind of Lutheran loyalty to the state.[108] As Leo himself had written a few months earlier: "A Jew should affirm the place in which he has been put, this means as a Jew among a non-Jewish people, and when the state makes him experience this with harshness, he must submit to it."[109] This harshness again became reality as Paul Leo lost his last part-time position, when the Lord Mayor Erich Gaertner banned him from entering the City Hospital as of August 17, 1935. This explanation was given: "With regard to your non-Aryan descent, I can no longer allow your further activity in the city institutions for the sick."[110]

105. Letter of Ernst Rolffs to the *Landeskirchenamt* from May 9, 1933, Archiv des Kirchenkreises Osnabrück, Personalakte Pastor Leo.

106. Letter of the *Landeskirchenamt* to Ernst Rolffs from August 28, 1933, Archiv des Kirchenkreises Osnabrück, Personalakte Pastor Leo.

107. Letter of Ernst Rolffs to the *Landeskirchenamt* from August 28, 1933, Archiv des Kirchenkreises Osnabrück, Personalakte Pastor Leo.

108. Ericksen, "Luther, Lutherans," 305–6.

109. Leo, "Denkschrift," 189–96n8. Reese, *Bekenntnis und Bekennen*, 412n87.

110. Letter of Erich Gaertner to Paul Leo from August 17, 1935, Archiv des Kirchenkreises Osnabrück, Personalakte Pastor Leo. "Städtische Krankenanstalten" (City Institutions for the Sick), meaning the City Hospital, the Teaching Institution for Midwifery, and the Children's Hospital.

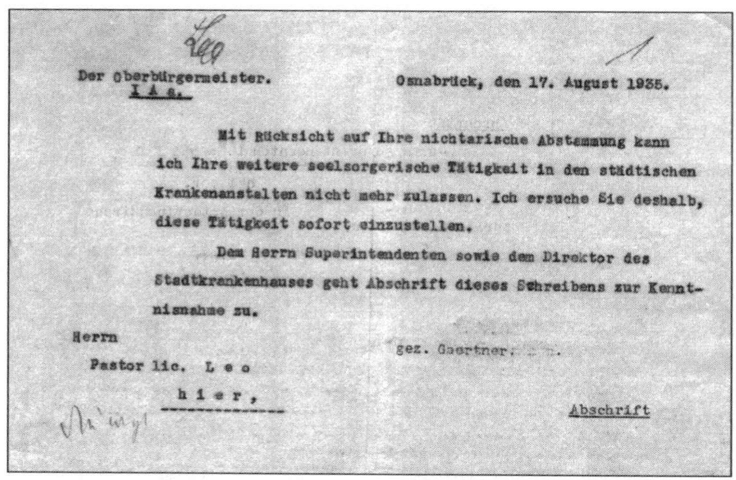

Leo

Der Oberbürgermeister.
I A 6.

Osnabrück, den 17. August 1935.

Mit Rücksicht auf Ihre nichtarische Abstammung kann ich Ihre weitere seelsorgerische Tätigkeit in den städtischen Krankenanstalten nicht mehr zulassen. Ich ersuche Sie deshalb, diese Tätigkeit sofort einzustellen.

Dem Herrn Superintendenten sowie dem Direktor des Stadtkrankenhauses geht Abschrift dieses Schreibens zur Kenntnisnahme zu.

Herrn
Pastor lic. L e o
h i e r ,

gez. Gaertner.

Abschrift

Dismissal of Paul Leo (August 17, 1935)

We have no documents concerning Paul Leo's direct reaction. However, a brief glimpse may be offered of the motives and relationships to the other actors: the Lord Mayor, the NSDAP district leader, and the pastors. For the first time, a dismissal of Paul Leo was openly connected with a breach of law, because the City Hospital actually was not run by the city of Osnabrück but was its own corporation. The domiciliary rights rested with the head of the City Hospital, Heinrich Fründ.[111] Fründ kept everything political away from the City Hospital; in 1936 his service was supervised by a Nazi doctor and in 1938 he was dismissed on a pretense.[112] A few days after the ban on Paul Leo, which really was legally ineffective, the Osnabrück NSDAP conducted an anti-Jewish rally.[113] The district leader of the NSDAP mentioned Paul Leo in his speech with one sentence: "We need no Jews any longer on our cattle yard and demand their dismissal in the same way as we have succeeded that Pastor Leo no

111. Heinrich Fründ (1880–1952).

112. Berger, *Wer bürgt für die Kosten?*, 254–55.

113. August 20, 1935. In the literature one finds the number at 25,000–30,000 participants. Cf. Kühling, *Die Juden in Osnabrück*, 87. Approximately 100,000 people lived at that time in Osnabrück.

longer is allowed to enter the hospital."[114] The name of this area leader was Wilhelm Münzer, who already in 1933 effectively determined at the District Church Assembly which laypersons were to be elected to the Lutheran District church council.

The ban issued by Erich Gaertner against Paul Leo irritated the Osnabrück pastors, since they supposed they had good relations with him. Ever since the Reformation, the city of Osnabrück had one representative on the church council of St. Mary. When Erich Gaertner became Lord Mayor in 1927, they were relieved that he personally would pay attention to the position. Gaertner was Evangelical-Reformed and the sentiment of the time was geared toward the separation of church and state. In fact, however, Erich Gaertner for years thereafter personally exercised his right to be seated and vote at the Lutheran church council of St. Mary.[115] Since 1933 Erich Gaertner's role was to guarantee that the interests of the NSDAP were sufficiently safeguarded.[116] For instance, the church council decided on April 20, 1933, that the church be used for an event to celebrate Hitler's birthday.[117] On Luther Day in November 1933, Erich Gaertner presented the main lecture.[118] Later an estrangement must have occurred, because Erich Gaertner left the church council of St. Mary in March 1935.[119]

When Leo received the letter of the Lord Mayor, Ernst Rolffs was just starting his vacation. Yet he still asked Hans Bodensieck,

114. Speech of Wilhelm Münzer, printed in *Osnabrücker Tagesblatt* (August 21, 1935).

115. Cf. the minutes of the church council meetings from 1927–35, Archiv des Kirchenkreises Osnabrück, Akte Kirchenvorstand St. Marien.

116. In documentation arranged by the church after the war, the wording states that Erich Gaertner's concern was "to present the desires of the Party." St. Mary Osnabrück, "Answers to the Questionnaire regarding the History of the Church from 1933 to the End of the War," gathered by Hans Bodensieck, October 1946, Landeskirchliches Archiv Hannover, S1 HII 916, Bl. 18–22.

117. Minutes of the church council from April 18, 1933, Archiv des Kirchenkreises Osnabrück, Akte Kirchenvorstand St. Marien.

118. *Osnabrücker Zeitung* (November 20, 1933).

119. Minutes of the church council from March 19, 1935, Archiv des Kirchenkreises Osnabrück, Akte Kirchenvorstand St. Marien.

as the substituting superintendent, to respond to the ban on Paul Leo.[120] Bodensieck composed a protest letter, which he circulated among all the other pastors for signing.[121] The letter ended with the sentence "in the name of all the pastors of St. Mary."[122] Exactly this led to the result that the pastors of the two other Osnabrück congregations, St. Catherine and the Luther Congregation, did not want to sign.[123] Frederick Bell added, "I can understand if members of a congregation for their own personal reasons decline the counseling of a non-Aryan."[124]

From this letter, which was finally sent, one notes that the activity of the counselor at the hospital was financed by the church and, according to the judgment of the mother superior of the City Hospital, Paul Leo rendered "counseling in an excellent way." In the future, the other pastors would not conduct church services "because of overwork" and would only visit the sick.[125] Erich Gaertner, to whom the letter was addressed, did not leave it unanswered, although his reply was in substance more a nonanswer, as one reads, "I do not want to discuss with you here the fundamental issue."[126] Concerning Hans Bodensieck's announcement that no other pastor would assume the church services in the City Hospital, Erich Gaertner asserted that he must understand this as

120. Letter of Ernst Rolffs to Hans Bodensieck from August 17, 1935, Archiv des Kirchenkreises Osnabrück, Personalakte Pastor Leo.

121. Letter of Hans Bodensieck to Erich Gaertner from August 20, 1935, Archiv des Kirchenkreises Osnabrück, Personalakte Pastor Leo.

122. Letter of Hans Bodensieck to Erich Gaertner from August 20, 1935, Archiv des Kirchenkreises Osnabrück, Personalakte Pastor Leo.

123. This can be deduced from the handwritten notes that the pastors formulated on the letter instead of signing it. Cf. Letter of Hans Bodensieck to Erich Gaertner from August 20, 1935, Archiv des Kirchenkreises Osnabrück, Personalakte Pastor Leo.

124. Letter of Hans Bodensieck to Erich Gaertner from August 20, 1935, Archiv des Kirchenkreises Osnabrück, Personalakte Pastor Leo.

125. Letter of Hans Bodensieck to Erich Gaertner from August 20, 1935, Archiv des Kirchenkreises Osnabrück, Personalakte Pastor Leo.

126. Letter of Erich Gaertner to Hans Bodensieck from August 26, 1935, Archiv des Kirchenkreises Osnabrück, Personalakte Pastor Leo.

"a conscious affront against the politics of the Nazis."[127] After that, the dialogue with the pastors finally ended.[128]

The *Landeskirchenamt* let the issue rest and thereafter the six pastors of St. Mary no longer acted in concert.[129] This shows that the "Osnabrück Circle" of Confessing pastors did not act any more in unison. The Confessing pastors, however, still acted individually. Concerning Johannes Bornschein,[130] one can read in the *Gestapo* documents the following sentence from his sermon on the date of September 22, 1935: "The Jews, yes, the Jews, we stand with them as we want. The Israelites are the chosen people of the Lord."[131] In the Osnabrück newspaper, a letter to the editor in September 1935 was published by Friedrich Grussendorf on the topic, "Is Christianity a Jewish Religion?"[132] His tenor was also that the Jews are God's chosen people.

The activity of Paul Leo in the City Hospital was then permanently finished. For the teaching institution of midwifery, however, there was a compromise. For baptisms in the hospital, the mother could select the pastor. Since Paul Leo as hospital counselor baptized for less money than the pastors of the congregations, a controversy arose in 1937: "I cannot comprehend that the members of the church council who belong to the NSDAP overlooked that the non-Aryan pastor is allowed to baptize for the cheap fee of 3 Marks (this includes, as Pastor Leo expressly affirmed to me today,

127. Letter of Erich Gaertner to Hans Bodensieck from August 26, 1935, Archiv des Kirchenkreises Osnabrück, Personalakte Pastor Leo.

128. Minutes from the meeting of the spiritual ministry (that is, a meeting of all Osnabrück pastors) from September 25, 1935, Archiv des Kirchenkreises Osnabrück, Personalakte Pastor Leo.

129. In September the pastors of St. Mary stated that the *Landeskirchenamt* should take action. But it did not become active. Cf. the minutes of the church council of St. Mary from September 9, 1935, Archiv des Kirchenkreises Osnabrück, Akte Kirchenvorstand St. Marien.

130. Johannes "Hans" Bornschein (born 1889) was pastor at St. Mary, Osnabrück, 1930–44.

131. Registry Card Johannes Bornschein, entry of the *Gestapo*-Osnabrück, Niedersächsische Staatsarchive, Außenstelle Osnabrück, Rep 439 Nr. 19.

132. Panayi, "Victims," 468.

even the baptisms which do not take place on the exact day when they were scheduled), while the Aryan pastors of congregations would require 10 Marks for the same official action."[133] Paul Leo's collegial relationship to the other special counselor, Paul Neumann, was stressed ever since 1935.[134] In 1936, Ernst Rolffs tried unsuccessfully through his friend Bishop August Marahrens to provide Paul Leo with a transfer to another position on account of his engagement for the Confessing Church.[135]

Once he was banned from the City Hospital in the summer of 1935, Paul Leo continued to suffer at the hands of the state administration. For example, in December 1935 he was confronted with the fact that according to new legislation his housekeeper was no longer allowed to work for a Jew. The Reformed Osnabrück pastor, Jacob Ites,[136] who was a friend of Paul Leo, tried to secure an exception[137] from the regional president of the government, Bernhard Eggers.[138] Bernhard Eggers answered that "unfortunately he is not in a situation to conduct any further action."[139]

Until his retirement in 1938, Paul Leo actually received support in Osnabrück from all six colleagues at St. Mary. These pastors, who like he himself belonged to the Confessing Church, convened

133. Letter of Frederick Bell to the church council of St. Catherine from January 14, 1937, Archiv des Kirchenkreises Osnabrück, Akte Gebühren.

134. Letter of Paul Neumann to Ernst Rolffs from July 2, 1936, Archiv des Kirchenkreises Osnabrück, Akte Bekennende Kirche.

135. Letter of Ernst Rolffs to August Marahrens from June 18, 1936, Archiv des Kirchenkreises Osnabrück, Akte Bekennende Kirche. August Marahrens declined the request. Cf. Letter of August Marahrens to Ernst Rolffs from June 18, 1936, Archiv des Kirchenkreises Osnabrück, Akte Bekennende Kirche.

136. Jacobus Ites (born 1872), Evangelical-Reformed pastor in Osnabrück (1902–38), member of the NSDAP.

137. Bernhard Eggers (1882–1937), regional president of the Government District of Osnabrück (1933–37).

138. Letter of Jacobus Ites to Bernhard Eggers from January 19, 1936, Niedersächsische Staatsarchive, Außenstelle Osnabrück, Rep. 430 Dez. 201. Acc. 16b/65 Nr. 44.

139. Letter of Bernhard Eggers to Jacobus Ites from January 23, 1936, Niedersächsische Staatsarchive, Außenstelle Osnabrück, Rep. 430 Dez. 201. Acc. 16b/65 Nr. 44.

several times in follow up to the Osnabrück Circle to prepare joint memoranda until 1938.[140] Since the paid part-time tasks ceased one after another, already in October 1934 the church council of St. Mary decided to underwrite the salary of Paul Leo.[141] Initially the entire corporation, the economic corporation of St. Catherine and the Luther Congregation, contributed to that. In 1936, that corporation reduced its subsidy but did not withdraw its support entirely.[142] The *Landeskirchenamt* thereafter paid subsidy, though the position of Paul Leo initially was supposed to finance itself.[143] Since Leo's salary at the initiative of St. Mary was paid from the congregational treasury, it was a matter of course that the church council of St. Mary looked to him for work. Since the beginning of 1935, this was to provide counseling in Haste.[144] Leo engaged this work with great energy. From 1935 to 1938, he conducted children's services there.[145] He had a group of confirmands and already in 1935 set his own date for confirmation in Haste.[146]

Paul Leo's engagement in Haste made great sense, since the small place was especially church oriented. A confessional Protestant primary school could continue to survive there even

140. Cf. the letters in the Archiv des Kirchenkreises Osnabrück, Akte Bekennende Kirche.

141. Decision of the church council from October 8, 1934, Archiv des Kirchenkreises Osnabrück, Akte Kirchenvorstand St. Marien. Letter of Franz Oldermann of September 3, 1936, Archiv des Kirchenkreises Osnabrück, Personalakte Pastor Leo.

142. Minutes of the church council of St. Mary from May 5, 1936, Archiv des Kirchenkreises Osnabrück, Personalakte Pastor Leo.

143. Letter of the *Landeskirchenamt* from December 21, 1936, Archiv des Kirchenkreises Osnabrück, Personalakte Pastor Leo.

144. Hellern, the considerably larger section of the city, initially belonged to Haste. Hellern belonged to the parish of Hans Bornschein and Haste to that of Friedrich Grußendorf. After 1936, Hellern can no longer be found in the sources. One finds it called "Haste-Lechtingen." See the Church Messenger from April 1938.

145. For about 10–20 children. Cf. the Church Messenger from January and April 1937.

146. Minutes of the church council of St. Mary from February 4, 1935, Archiv des Kirchenkreises Osnabrück, Akte Kirchenvorstand St. Marien.

until 1945. By contrast, beginning in 1933 the Nazi-dominated Osnabrück city administration built as prestige projects three housing settlements with one of them in Haste.[147] Therefore, while Paul Leo was welcomed by the church-oriented people in Haste, he was only tolerated by the newcomers. After some time, children's services and confirmation classes had to be transferred from a restaurant in Haste to a less public place.[148] The use of the Protestant primary school in Haste was prohibited by the government presidium.[149] Thereafter, church services were held in the chapel of the Catholic monastery in Haste.[150]

Paul Leo was especially dedicated to planning for a new chapel in Haste.[151] To get ideas for the interior of the chapel he visited a church art exhibition in Hanover in 1937, where he met the sculptor Eva Dittrich. Dittrich hailed from a long ancestry of pastors.[152] They talked with one another about church art and a friendship ensued.[153] The building of the chapel was supported by the church council of St. Mary. A high point occurred in 1937, when in May they held and successfully completed a fund drive. At its conclusion, the church council expressly stated that it would continue with the building of the chapel in Haste.[154] From the side of the state this project met with suspicion.[155] The *Landeskirch-*

147. *Osnabrücker Tageblatt* (January 30, 1937).

148. Church Messenger from June 1937.

149. Church council meeting of St. Mary from May 4, 1937, Archiv des Kirchenkreises Osnabrück, Akte Kirchenvorstand St. Marien.

150. Church council meeting of St. Mary from May 4, 1937, Archiv des Kirchenkreises Osnabrück, Akte Kirchenvorstand St. Marien.

151. Minutes of the church council of St. Mary from March 19, 1935, Archiv des Kirchenkreises Osnabrück, Akte Kirchenvorstand St. Marien.

152. Her grandfather was the Stettin Councilor Julius Dittrich (1823–83); her father was Johannes Dittrich, Superintendent in Diepholz (1900–1906) and Superintendent in Lesum near Bremen (1906–23).

153. Leo, "Biographie Paul Leos," n37. Later both celebrated June 1 as the date when they became acquainted.

154. Minutes of the church council of St. Mary from September 14, 1937, Archiv des Kirchenkreises Osnabrück, Akte Kirchenvorstand St. Marien.

155. The Osnabrück *Gestapo* document concerning the pastors of St.

enamt also expected in August 1937 that Paul Leo should account for all the collected money.[156] The project of building the chapel was finally terminated in March 1938, when the city administration refused to issue a building permit and the *Gestapo* froze the account of the congregation.[157] Thereafter Paul Leo's activity as pastor of the church came to a rapid conclusion.

The period leading to his formal retirement from office as pastor followed forthwith. At the beginning of April 1938, Paul Leo reported in person to the *Landeskirchenamt* about his professional activity. What exactly he said has not been preserved. The *Landeskirchenamt* reacted quickly and wrote to Ernst Rolffs: "Pastor Lic. Leo has reported here about the great difficulties which oppose his further activity in Osnabrück."[158] They proposed that Paul Leo would be placed into "temporary retirement."[159] The church had introduced this form of retirement only on March 6, 1937. The rationale given was that "there were conflicts in the respective congregations which disallowed a further stay there and similar difficulties were to be expected in other congregations."[160] Ernst Rolffs answered: "I must confirm to my regret the oral report of pastor Lic. Leo about the difficulties that grew out of his activity

---

Mary: "since 1935 they continuously transgressed against the law of collections by collecting money for building a new chapel." Niedersächsische Staatsarchive, Außenstelle Osnabrück, Rep 439 Nr 19 Eingangskartei der Gestapo-Osnabrück.

156. Letter of the *Landeskirchenamt* to Ernst Rolffs from August 27, 1937, Archiv des Kirchenkreises Osnabrück, Personalakte Pastor Leo.

157. Minutes of the church council of St. Mary from March 25, 1938, Archiv des Kirchenkreises Osnabrück, Akte Kirchenvorstand St. Marien. Letter of Hans Bodensieck to the *Landeskirchenamt* from July 19, 1939, Archiv des Kirchenkreises Osnabrück, Akte Staatspolizeiliche Maßnahmen.

158. *Landeskirchenamt* to Ernst Rolffs from April 4, 1938, Archiv des Kirchenkreises Osnabrück, Personalakte Pastor Leo.

159. *Landeskirchenamt* to Ernst Rolffs from April 4, 1938, Archiv des Kirchenkreises Osnabrück, Personalakte Pastor Leo.

160. Hans Otte, Communication from Landeskirchlichen Archiv Hannover 2 (November 2003), 21. Since this kind of retirement was only used for Jewish pastors, Otte commented this was a "hidden Aryan paragraph." Cf. Lindemann, "Typisch jüdisch," 564.

here."[161] He emphasized that in Haste Paul Leo has "the trust of all church-minded people."[162] However, "from the political side pressure is being exerted upon him."[163] He recommended that Paul Leo be placed into temporary retirement. Before the beginning of May 1938, the Osnabrück superintendent general and the executive committee of pastors agreed to temporary retirement.[164]

On May 18, 1938, Paul Leo received a letter from the *Landeskirchenamt*, which stated that his "further activity"[165] as pastor was no longer possible and closed with the suggestion: "Before we pursue further action, we advise you to apply for temporary retirement."[166] However, the church council of St. Mary already knew by the middle of April 1938 about Paul Leo's application.[167] It issued the following declaration: "The church council expressly states that there were no reasons connected with the performance of his work that caused him to leave his duties. The church council regrets therefore his departure and thanks Pastor Leo for his faithful and dedicated work through which the congregational life in Haste was considerably enhanced."[168] On Easter Monday, April 18,

161. Ernst Rolffs to the *Landeskirchenamt* from April 5, 1938, Archiv des Kirchenkreises Osnabrück, Personalakte Pastor Leo.

162. Ernst Rolffs to the *Landeskirchenamt* from April 5, 1938, Archiv des Kirchenkreises Osnabrück, Personalakte Pastor Leo.

163. Ernst Rolffs to the *Landeskirchenamt* from April 5, 1938, Archiv des Kirchenkreises Osnabrück, Personalakte Pastor Leo.

164. Ernst Rolffs to the *Landeskirchenamt* from April 16, 1938, Archiv des Kirchenkreises Osnabrück, Personalakte Pastor Leo. *Landeskirchenamt* to Ernst Rolffs from May 6, 1938, Archiv des Kirchenkreises Osnabrück, Personalakte Pastor Leo.

165. Letter of the *Landeskirchenamt* to Paul Leo from May 18, 1938, Archiv des Kirchenkreises Osnabrück, Personalakte Pastor Leo.

166. Letter of the *Landeskirchenamt* to Paul Leo from May 18, 1938, Archiv des Kirchenkreises Osnabrück, Personalakte Pastor Leo.

167. "The church council acknowledged the application of Pastor Leo to be placed in temporary retirement." Minutes of the church council of St. Mary from April 22, 1938, Archiv des Kirchenkreises Osnabrück, Personalakte Pastor Leo.

168. Minutes of the church council of St. Mary from April 22, 1938, Archiv des Kirchenkreises Osnabrück, Personalakte Pastor Leo.

1938, Paul Leo officiated for the last time as pastor of the church. This day was confirmation,[169] which presumably again was in Haste for Paul Leo's confirmands. Most likely, he was placed into temporary retirement on August 1, 1938.[170]

Since the end of April 1938, Paul Leo spent several weeks on a relaxing vacation in the hotel Schloss Schaumburg near Rinteln. Was it by accident that the hotel was situated in the congregational parish of the last remaining Jewish pastor of the church of Hanover, Gustav Oehlert? Did they meet each other there to talk about the situation?[171]

Paul Leo wrote to Ernst Rolffs: "Since I have arrived here, I really notice how completely I am at the end of my nerves."[172] Exactly at the official start of his retirement in August 1938, he vacated his official living quarters.[173] Around the time of Paul Leo's last workday, they had developed an ecclesial procedure. On April 28, 1938, the *Landeskirchenamt* decreed that all pastors had to pledge an oath of allegiance to Hitler, the text of which already had irritated the accommodating Osnabrück confessional pastors: "I swear by God, the almighty and all-knowing: I will be faithful

169. Minutes of the church council of St. Mary from April 22, 1938, Archiv des Kirchenkreises Osnabrück, Personalakte Pastor Leo.

170. Letter of the *Landeskirchenamt* to Paul Leo from June 20, 1938, Archiv des Kirchenkreises Osnabrück, Personalakte Pastor Leo. It could not be detected why the *Landeskirchenamt* set the beginning of temporary retirement for April 1, 1938, to calculate the compensation. Cf. *Landeskirchenamt Hannover*, "Calculation of the Pension Payments of Paul Leo" from April 15, 1938, Landeskirchliches Archiv Hannover, N 147, Entschädigungssache Paul Leo.

171. Somewhat later the *Landeskirchenamt* received "a report from the Tinteln church council that positively valued Oehlert's teaching and noted his gift of preaching." Hans Otter, Mitteilungen aus dem Landeskirchlichen Archiv Hannover 2 (November 2003), 21.

172. Letter of Paul Leo to Ernst Rolffs from May 13, 1938, Archiv des Kirchenkreises Osnabrück, Personalakte Pastor Leo.

173. Paul Leo was registered from October 10, 1930, to July 27, 1938, at Kanzlerwall 8 and since July 28, 1938, at Bohmter Street 38, fourth floor. Cf. Registration Certificate of the City of Osnabrück from May 6, 1958, Landeskirchliches Archiv Hannover, N 147, Entschädigungssache Paul Leo. Document by Carl Siegert to the Gestapo-Osnabrück of December 22, 1938, Landeskirchliches Archiv Hannover, N 147, Entschädigungssache Paul Leo, n9.

and obedient to the leader of the German Reich and of the people, Adolf Hitler, to obey the laws and conscientiously to fulfill my obligations in office, as truly as God helps me!"[174]

At the next gathering of all Osnabrück pastors, there was "a very lively discussion."[175] Ernst Rolffs reported to the *Landeskirchenamt* that they did not succeed "to overcome the scruples of a number of brothers and achieve agreement."[176] Even at a later meeting of the Confessing pastors alone they were not unanimous. "Grussendorf ranted courageously in his usual manner, though that made no impression on Karwehl because of the deficient theology. . . . I will now attempt to talk with Leo and Grussendorf and then tomorrow we will together place Karwehl under the fire."[177] Since the middle of July 1938, the *Landeskirchenamt* no longer demanded the oath and the issue dissipated.[178]

Arrest and Emigration

On November 9, 1938, there occurred also in Osnabrück the usual official festivities of the SS (*Schutzstaffel*: Hitler's combat troop) and representatives of other Nazi organizations to remember the failed coup (by Hitler) from 1923, this time at the City Hall.[179] Af-

174. The text of the oath that was to be sworn. Archiv des Kirchenkreises Emsland Bentheim, Fasz Az. 10/161.

175. Report of May 19, 1938, on the gathering of May 18, 1938, Archiv des Kirchenkreises Osnabrück, Akte Konvent.

176. Report of May 19, 1938, on the gathering of May 18, 1938, Archiv des Kirchenkreises Osnabrück, Akte Konvent.

177. Letter of Hans Bornschein to Heinrich Brandt from June 6, 1938, Landeskirchliches Archiv Hannover, Registratur der Landessuperintendentur des Sprengels Osnabrück-Diepholz "Pfarrer und Pfarramt Osnabrück: Allgemeines" Jahr 1938.

178. In October 1938, three Osnabrück pastors still had not yet pledged their oath. Cf. *Landeskirchenamt Hannover* to Ernst Rolffs from October 21, 1938, Landeskirchliches Archiv Hannover, Registratur der Landessuperintendentur des Sprengels Osnabrück-Diepholz "Pfarrer und Pfarramt Osnabrück: Allgemeines" Jahr 1938.

179. "Osnabrück remembers the dead of November 9. Festive Memorial in the City Hall for those who died for the movement," *Osnabrück Tageblatt* (November 10, 1938).

terwards, "the participants visited the surrounding restaurants and bars"[180] and convened again at about one o'clock in the morning in front of St. Mary and subsequently in small parties to "terrorize Jewish families and take the men into custody."[181]

Paul Leo's daughter Anna remembers: "It was the end. And the beginning of everything. That night they took Vati away."[182] In the middle of the night men stood in front of the door: "The night had been like any other. Vati had come to say prayers with her. . . . Suddenly she woke. Shouting and banging on the front door. . . . More shouting and pounding. Finally, heavy boots in the hallway. 'Come with us. Immediately!'"[183]

Eva Leo, who herself was not there, reported: "In the night of November 9 some SS-men rapped at the door, demanding that Paul should come with them. The housekeeper got up, awakened Paul who did not even get the time to get dressed. Fortunately, Miss Koch had the presence of her mind to grab his coat to wear over the pajamas."[184]

Just like the other thirty-seven male Jews who had been brought there from Osnabrück and surroundings, Paul Leo was housed for some time in the basement of the western wing of the

180. Weitkamp, "Hochmut und Fall," 257.

181. Weitkamp, "Hochmut und Fall," 257n179. Brief reports of the event are given in Weitkamp, "Der Sicherheitsdienst," 222; Röhm and Thierfelder, *Juden*, 494n28.

182. Cf. Leo Ellis, "Last Stop, Prickly Pear," 1. Paul Leo's daughter Anna was only eight years old and wrote this down decades later. However, she was a direct witness.

183. Leo Ellis, "Last Stop, Prickly Pear," 1n181.

184. Leo, "Biographie Paul Leos," n37. Brandy has pointed out the incorrect date (correct is the early morning of November 10, 1938). Cf. Brandy, "Gustav Oehlert und Paul Leo," 219. Also, the identification of the perpetrators as "S.S. men" seems doubtful. A participation of the SS occurred only after this night. The groups that conducted the seizures consisted of members of the SA. Cf. Weitkamp, "Hochmut und Fall," 257–63n179.

Osnabrück Castle,[185] to be transferred on November 11 or 12, 1938, to the concentration camp Buchenwald.[186]

Paul Leo may have kept the exact events in the concentration camp forever to himself.[187] Only a few notes are preserved regarding his incarceration, which will be summarized in what follows.

His daughter, Anna, wrote: "'Vati, tell us about Buchenwald. What was it like?' 'I can't talk about it, Liebchen (my dear one), and you mustn't ask. I don't dare tell you the terrible things that happened. For the sake of our safety, I must keep quiet.'"[188]

Similarly, the account of the son of Paul Leo's colleague, Hans Rapp, wrote: "He returned after the concentration camp incarceration. When my father asked him about details, he refused any answer. He had to sign that he will not divulge anything of his incarceration either in public or even privately, otherwise he would be immediately returned."[189]

The Osnabrück pastor Hans Bodensieck noted later: "He conducted devotions in the overflowing concentration camp in a corner for Christian non-Aryans with their most avid participation and also of Jews."[190]

185. Cf. Weitkamp, "Hochmut und Fall," 263n179. Weitkamp, "Hochmut und Fall," 222n180. Junk and Sellmeyer, *Stationen auf dem Weg*, 256n83. St. Marien-Osnabrück. Antworten zum Fragebogen zur Geschichte der Landeskirche von 1933 bis zum Kriegsende, composed by Hans Bodensieck, October 1946, Landeskirchliches Archiv Hannover, S1 HIII 916, Bl. 18–22. Bodensieck mentioned that Paul Leo was charged there "with very degrading work" (Cf. St. Marien-Osnabrück. Antworten zum Fragebogen zur Geschichte der Landeskirche von 1933 bis zum Kriegsende, composed by Hans Bodensieck, October 1946, Landeskirchliches Archiv Hannover, S1 HIII 916, Bl. 18–22). It may have been that some of the convicts were charged with the cleaning of the rooms and the toilets (cf. Junk and Sellmeyer, *Stationen auf dem Weg*, 119n82). Beyond this, there are no reports that the inmates were mistreated. Weitkamp, "Hochmut und Fall," 258n179.

186. On November 11, 1938, there was one transport and on the following day two transports. Weitkamp, "Hochmut und Fall," 259n179.

187. This was a typical conduct of former inmates. Cf. Wagner, *Die Gestapo war nicht allein*, 31.

188. Leo Ellis, "Last Stop, Prickly Pear," 4n181.

189. Communication of Hans Reinhard Rapp from June 10, 2013.

190. St. Marien-Osnabrück. Antworten zum Fragebogen zur Geschichte der

Eva Leo observed: "At an unnoticed place he used to gather some of the other inmates, Jews and non-Jews, talking to them about what he had learned through his study of theology: bearing one's cross joyfully and patiently."[191]

A large part of those Jews who were taken into custody over the course of November 9, 1938, were again released from the concentration camp. Receiving a confirmation to emigrate then increased the speed. Soon after November 9, 1938, the embassy in the Netherlands opened an additional separate office in Berlin, operated by one person, that generously issued visas in advance for those who were incarcerated. Paul Leo was among the first ones to receive a visa.[192] The release of Paul Leo was closely connected with the issuing of this visa and his family knew already before Christmas that he would receive a visa.[193] On December 29, 1938, he was again a free person and back in Osnabrück.[194]

Landeskirche von 1933 bis zum Kriegsende, composed by Hans Bodensieck, October 1946, Landeskirchliches Archiv Hannover, S1 HIII 916, Bl. 18–22.

191. Leo, "Biographie Paul Leos," n37.

192. Röhm and Thierfelder, *Juden*, 259.

193. "According to a communication which I received today from relatives of my son-in-law a visa, a so-called permit, is to be expected in the immediate future for my son-in-law and his daughter to enter England." Document by Carl Siegert to the Gestapo-Osnabrück of December 22, 1938, Landeskirchliches Archiv Hannover, N 147, Entschädigungssache Paul Leo, n9.

194. Telegram of Paul Leo to Hans Schenk from December 29, 1938, Landeskirchliches Archiv Hannover, N 147 Entschädigungssache Paul Leo.

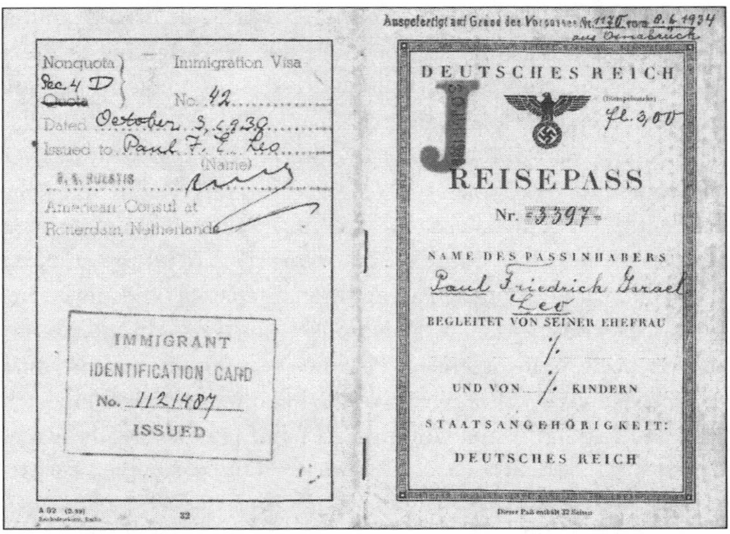

Nonquota } Immigration Visa
Sec. 4 D
~~Quota~~
No. 42
Issued to Paul F. L. Leo
(Name)
American Consul at
Rotterdam, Netherlands

IMMIGRANT
IDENTIFICATION CARD
No. 1121487
ISSUED

DEUTSCHES REICH
J
fl. 3,00
REISEPASS
Nr. 3397
NAME DES PASSINHABERS
Paul Friedrich Israel Leo
BEGLEITET VON SEINER EHEFRAU
./.
UND VON ./. KINDERN
STAATSANGEHÖRIGKEIT:
DEUTSCHES REICH

Paul Leo Passport with Visa (Categorized as "Jew")

On January 4, 1939, Paul Leo sent his daughter Anna on a train to the Netherlands.[195] She remembers: "Vati had said the train was just for children who were Jewish or Jewish Christian."[196] With other Jewish children she came into a children's home at Losser. In the school in Osnabrück she had been called a "Jewish Schickse."[197] Now she was confronted with the question from other Jewish girls of her age: "You're not a Jew. Why are you here?"[198] For Paul Leo, too, it was decided at the beginning of January 1939 that he would soon emigrate.[199] He gave the power of attorney for his

195. Letter of Carl Siegert to Hans Schenk from January 6, 1939, Landeskirchliches Archiv Hannover, S1 HII 920, Nachlass Prof. Lic. Paul Leo.

196. Leo Ellis, "Last Stop, Prickly Pear," 11n181. The transportation of the children and the stay in the home for children were organized and financed by "Comité voor Joodsche Vluchtelingen."

197. Leo, "Biographie Paul Leos," n37.

198. Leo Ellis, "Last Stop, Prickly Pear," 13n181.

199. Letter of Martin Albertz to Paul Leo from January 10, 1939, in Röhm and Thierfelder, *Juden*, 343–44n180. Letter of Carl Siegert to Hans Schenk from January 6, 1939, Landeskirchliches Archiv Hannover, S1 HII 920,

bank account to Helene Leo, the wife of his brother Ulrich, so they could pay the cost for the dissolution of his housing.[200]

Jud Leo vereinnahmt Kirchensteuer

Unter den Juden, die ihrer staatsfeindlichen Umtriebe wegen Aufenthalt in einem Konzentrationslager genommen haben, befindet sich auch der 46jährige Jude **Paul Leo** aus Göttingen. Er gehört zu jenen ganz Schlauen, die einen Höhepunkt der Tarnungskunst zu erklimmen dachten, wenn sie die Laufbahn eines — christlich-evangelischen Pastors einschlugen. In der Systemzeit predigte er an den verschiedensten Stellen „Gottes Wort" — wie er es verstand. Die nationalsozialistische Erhebung fand ihn auf dem wohldotierten Pöstchen eines Anstaltspfarrers in staatlichen Anstalten zu **Osnabrück**.

Nachdem er aus diesem Schlupfwinkel vertrieben worden war, zeigte ihm die Evangelische Kirche nicht etwa die kalte Schulter, sondern — sie übertrug ihm einen Seelsorgerbezirk in **Haste**, einem Vorort von Kassel. Erst als auch bei der dortigen Bevölkerung seine rassische Zugehörigkeit ruchbar wurde und sie sich dagegen auflehnte, von einem Volljuden „seelsorgerisch" betreut zu werden, bequemten sich die kirchlichen Oberen dazu, dieses Prunkstück in den Ruhestand zu schicken.

Wohlbemerkt: in den Ruhestand. Das hat zur Folge, daß an jedem Monatsersten an der Pforte des Konzentrationslagers der Geldbriefträger erscheint, um diesem rüstigen und arbeitsfähigen Juden ein „Ruhegehalt" von sage und schreibe 400 RM. auszuzahlen, das ihm die Evangelische Landeskirche der Provinz Hannover treu und brav aus den Mitteln der Kirchensteuerzahler überweist.

Wie viele arme Volksgenossen müssen wohl von den Kirchensteuerämtern drangsaliert, bedroht oder gar gepfändet werden, ehe die Evangelische Landeskirche in Hannover ihre 400 RM. monatlich für einen arbeitsscheuen und staatsfeindlichen Juden beisammen hat! Wie angenehm ist es für die eifrigen Kirchensteuerzahler, zu wissen, daß sie während der Laufbahn dieses Juden schon ein Vermögen aufbringen mußten, um die zerstörende Wirkung zu finanzieren, die Individuen vom Schlage des Juden Leo in der Evangelischen Kirche ausgeübt haben, so daß aus ihr schließlich das wurde, was sie heute ist —: ein Trümmerhaufen. Nichts spricht deutlicher für die geradezu unmögliche Stellung der Kirche in der Volksgemeinschaft als dieser symbolische Zustand:

Der Staat sperrt einen verbrecherischen Juden ein, die Kirche bedenkt den gleichen Juden mit Geschenken aus Mitteln, die sie mit Hilfe des Staates eintreibt.

Propaganda News Article about "Jew Leo" (January 22, 1939)

The incarceration of Paul Leo had another consequence. On January 19, 1938, in the SS Journal *Das Schwarze Korps* (The Black Corps), an article appeared entitled "Jew Leo Cashes In on Church Tax" and on January 22, 1939, there was a brief article in the two Osnabrück daily papers under the headline "Jew Leo Cashes Church Tax," which stated that Paul Leo as a Jew and a concentration camp inmate received a salary.[201] These were the

---

Nachlass Prof. Lic. Paul Leo.

200. Deposition of Helene Leo at the District Court in Bremen from July 22, 1966, Landeskirchliches Archiv Hannover, N 147, Entschädigungssache Paul Leo.

201. *Das Schwarze Korps* from January 19,1939. *Neue Volkszeitung* (January 22, 1939), Niedersächsische Staatsarchive, Außenstelle Osnabrück, Dep 3b XVI Nr. 9. *Osnabrücker Tageblatt* (January 22, 1939). After the injunctions,

typical hate articles during the Nazi period. The *Landeskirchenamt* was quick to announce that Leo had not received retirement pay in the concentration camp, but it had been transferred to his checking account at the postal office "as it is customary for those Jews who have been removed from state service."[202] On February 2, 1939, Leo traveled to the Netherlands, where he found lodgings in a refugee home.[203] In October 1939, he visited his daughter in the refugee home for children in Losser and a week later he travelled with her by sea to the USA.[204]

---

these were the only remaining Osnabrück daily papers. In the SS-association magazine, *Das Schwarze Korps*, another similar article appeared in February 1939. Cf. Brandy, "Gustav Oehlert und Paul Leo," 220–23n183. Röhm and Thierfelder, *Juden*, 343–44n180. Joachim Maßner, "Paul Friedrich Leo," 180–81. Kühling, *Osnabrück*, 88.

202. Letter of the *Landeskirchenamt* to the Superintendents of the seat of the Land Superintendent Osnabrück from January 27, 1939, Archiv des Kirchenkreises Emsland-Bentheim, Fasz Az. 10/161.

203. Letter of Paul Leo to the "Vorläufige Kirchenleitung" (Temporary Church Board) of the Confessing Church from February 6, 1939, in Röhm and Thierfelder, *Juden*, 290–91n180. Entschädigungsantrag of Eva Leo from March 12, 1958, Landeskirchliches Archiv Hannover, N 147, Entschädigungssache Paul Leo.

204. Eva Leo, hand-written CV of Paul Leo of May 12, 1958. Application for compensation of Eva Leo from March 12, 1958, Landeskirchliches Archiv Hannover, N 147, Entschädigungssache Paul Leo. According to other sources, he journeyed via Great Britain to the USA. Most likely it was only a stay on the boat in an English harbor.

Remembrance Plaque in Norderney, Germany, P. Leo. Name Restored after Removal by Nazis

Street Sign in Osnabrück, Germany with Memorial

Paul and Eva Leo Family

2

Life Stations in the United States (1939–58)[1]

"The fear that the Holocaust in Germany under Hitler may be forgotten or not be taken seriously gives me incentive to write about my late husband's experiences in Nazi Germany and about our immigration."[2] So wrote Eva Leo in the opening sentence of her autobiographical reflections, including life together with her husband, Paul. Paul Leo was the descendent of a prominent Jewish lineage in the line of Moses Mendelssohn, the renowned philosopher. He was the great grandnephew of Felix Mendelssohn-Bartholdy, the famous nineteenth-century composer, and the great grandson of Fanny Hensel (née Mendelsohn-Bartholdy), the composer and pianist.

As this book describes, the persecution of those with Jewish ancestry, even those baptized as Christians and serving as pastors in Christian ministry, was relentless in Germany in the 1930s, escalating toward the "Final Solution." Daniel Jonah Goldhagen has identified five characteristics of genocide, what he names "eliminationism": (1) Transformation—the destruction of a group's core identities; (2) Repression—the control of the scapegoated people by restricting movement and intimidation; (3) Expulsion—the deportation of hated people into other lands,

1. Chapters 2 and 3 by Craig L. Nessan.

2. Leo, "Autobiographical Notes," 1.

designated territories, or camps; (4) Prevention of Reproduction—measures to restrict or interrupt normal biological reproduction; and (5) Extermination—the killing of the identified victims.[3] These "are different technical solutions to the perceived problem of dealing with unwanted or putatively threatening groups, to fulfilling the most fundamental desire of somehow getting rid of such groups, which Germans emblematically expressed in one of the most frequent rallying cries before and during the Nazi period: 'Juden raus' (Jews out)."[4]

Given the circumstances of Leo's arrest and imprisonment, especially following *Kristallnacht* during the night of November 9–10, 1938 (the night before Luther's birthdate), it is a miracle that events allowed the possibility of his emigration at all. Officers from the SS (*Schutzstaffel*: "Protection Squadron") took Leo into custody during that night. He arrived as a prisoner at the Buchenwald concentration camp, from which he was allowed only to write an occasional postcard, alerting his family that he was still alive. Leo benefitted from the intervention of Hermann Maas, who employed his influence to secure exit visas for many Jewish people in the late 1930s and early 1940s.[5]

After several weeks Leo was released from Buchenwald under the condition that he must leave Germany within two months. Upon his release from Buchenwald, Leo had lost considerable weight and was suffering illness. While in the concentration camp, he had not been tortured but had been subjected to severe deprivation, humiliating work, and physical cruelty. Nevertheless, Leo organized theological and pastoral conversations at Buchenwald to encourage other inmates in their struggles. These circumstances made it necessary for Leo to make plans to leave Germany with his young daughter Anna (born 1931).

3. Goldhagen, *Worse Than War*, 14–18.

4. Goldhagen, *Worse Than War*, 19.

5. On July 28, 1964, Yad Vashem recognized the Reverend Hermann Maas (1877–1970) as one of the "Righteous Among the Nations."

Passport Photo of Paul Leo (January 1939)

Passport Photo of Anna Leo (January 1939)

Emigration in 1939

Leo's brother, Ulrich (a philologian by occupation), had emigrated from Germany to Venezuela some months earlier, where he had obtained a position as "exterior minister" through the mediation of friends. Ulrich's wife and two sons had remained behind at the family home near Frankfurt/Main to prepare their belongings for shipping. At that time the children of Ulrich and his wife attended a Quaker school in Holland, in order to spare them from the Nazi indoctrination that prevailed in the German schools. On January 9, 1939, the SS magazine *Das Schwarze Korps* published an article reviling Leo. Knowing about circumstances in the Netherlands from his brother, he immediately sent his daughter Anna there on a children's transport to live in a Jewish children's home.[6]

Leo prepared a few possessions—one suitcase of clothes, a box of books, typewriter, and DM 20—and set out with his emigration papers for a refugee camp in the Netherlands. "When his train crossed the border, he did not know that he would never cross the border again."[7] The typewriter was taken from him at the border by the customs officer.[8] Once at the camp, Leo began to minister to the other refugees. "His ability to listen, to comfort, to find the right word at the right time—let him forget his own sorrow; and by bearing the burden of all the others he fulfilled the law of him under whose service he had put his life."[9]

Life in the children's home was extremely difficult for Anne. Having been bullied and called names by Aryan classmates in Germany, now she was the only child raised Christian among many Jewish children. "When her father visited her, he found her in tears, a rare thing for a child with her stable and sensible qualities."[10] However, at the refugee camp where Leo was staying, there was no place for her to stay. Arrangements were made for

6. Leo, "Autobiographical Notes," 4.

7. Leo, "Autobiographical Notes," 4.

8. Bodensieck, "His Times Were in God's Hands," 11.

9. Leo, "Autobiographical Notes," 4.

10. Leo, "Autobiographical Notes," 5.

a Dutch couple, who had no children, to take Anna into their home, where she had her own room and was treated like a member of their family.

During his pastorate at Hannover in 1937, Leo had become acquainted with the artist Eva Dittrich (1901–98), meeting her at a traveling exhibit of church art. Because Leo was involved with plans for building a chapel, he attended this exhibition to gather ideas for this project. Leo and Dittrich engaged in lively conversation about contemporary church art. After the conclusion of the exhibit, the two continued corresponding.

Eva Dittrich attended high school in Bremen, and, after a year as an *au pair* for her oldest sister, she attended the College of the Arts and Crafts in Bremen, studying porcelain painting.[11] Her father was regional bishop of the Evangelical (Lutheran) Church. Upon completing her studies in Bremen, she was accepted as an apprentice with Friedrich Harjes (1888–1952), a metal sculptor in Burgdam. She also briefly studied art with Wilhelm Groß (1883–1974), a wood sculptor and woodcut artist, in Eden near Oranienburg. In 1932 she finished her master's degree at Hildesheim, becoming the first female Master Metal Sculptor in Germany. With meager resources Dittrich established a workshop in Hildesheim, working as a freelance sculptor. She accepted commissions from churches and church architects such as Rudolf Jäger (1903–78), creating baptismal fonts, communion ware, crucifixes, candlesticks, lamps, and reliefs (representational art) depicting biblical themes.[12]

11. For this and the following, see "German Metal Sculptor: Eva Leo."

12. On Eva Dittrich's education in the 1930s, see "Eva Leo" on Wikipedia.

Friedrich Harjes with Eva Dittrich among Students

Workshop of Friedrich Harjes

Out of concern for Dittrich's wellbeing, Leo had offered to end their correspondence in mid-1939 due to his being persecuted for his Jewish ancestry, because this could also cause her difficulties with the Nazis. Dittrich refused and continued the relationship, becoming alarmed at the discovery of his arrest and internment at Buchenwald. She remained in occasional contact with Leo's mother and sister-in-law, remembering fondly their friendship and theological discussions. Dittrich wrote about her relationship with Leo: "Only once—after I had not heard from him for a longer period than usual—I wrote a short note to him, wondering whether our relationship might not be a *burden* to him. There came an immediate answer that our relationship was as much a burden to him as a blossoming cherry tree in the springtime. Then I knew. But we never again mentioned it, neither one of us."[13]

During Leo's time in the Netherlands, Leo and Dittrich continued their correspondence, taking all precautions not to draw unwanted attention to themselves under the conditions of censorship. Leo's sister-in-law invited Dittrich to a meeting at the medieval castle at Schaumburg between Hildesheim and Osnabrück. There Dittrich received an envelope that contained a poem in Leo's handwriting and a small geranium blossom. The contents overwhelmed Dittrich. She understood that this was a proposal that she leave her family and work, "which had just started to be known and recognized in Germany."[14] In this way Leo was asking her whether she was willing to leave her homeland and "like Abraham follow the call" that now came to her. After some time for reflection at the castle, Dittrich gave word that she would accept the proposal.

Dittrich prepared herself to depart at the opportune time. She had previously secured her passport, anticipating a possible escape. The preparations were complicated by conditions in the camp and the lack of permission to get married in the Netherlands as a neutral country (which marriage in any case would have been illegal in Germany). On May 12 Dittrich met Leo in

13. Leo, "Autobiographical Notes," 6.

14. For this and the following quote, Leo, "Autobiographical Notes," 7.

Amsterdam, staying with his sister-in-law, who together with her children was waiting to join her husband in Venezuela. When asked by the SS officers on the train, Dittrich explained her travel as part of her work as an artist. After some precious time together in the city, she returned to her studio and waited, burying herself in artwork to pass the time. Germany was expanding its territory country by country. Over time, the repression of the population by the Nazi regime increased in intensity.

Finally, on August 26 Dittrich received a telegram from the sister-in-law stating, "Come immediately." She confided her plan to leave to a trusted friend, who helped her pack two suitcases with clothing and books. Dittrich left Germany on August 30 (two days before Germany's attack on Poland started World War II) on a round-trip ticket to Amsterdam, supposedly a "weekend trip" not to arouse suspicion. When she arrived by train in Amsterdam, Dittrich went to stay with Leo's sister-in-law, who had not been expecting her sudden appearance.

Two days later the welcome news came that Leo's friend, Otto Piper—who earlier had emigrated from Germany on account of his Jewish wife and now was teaching New Testament at Princeton Theological Seminary—had arranged a teaching position for Leo in the United States. While Leo and his daughter Anna easily secured their visas, it was unclear how long Dittrich might have to wait. Based on US quotas, she might have had to wait for up to ten years. However, alternative plans were quickly made for Dittrich to sail with Leo's sister-in-law and children to Venezuela on October 12. This was the same day that Leo and Anna departed by ship to the United States.

Pittsburgh, Pennsylvania

On July 15, 1938, the American Section of the Lutheran World Convention had established a formal working agreement with the Protestant agency The American Committee for German Christian Refugees. Two key leaders were Frederick Knubel, chair of the American Section, and Ralph Long, member of the

Executive Committee. There was a commitment by Lutherans to open an office for the support and resettlement of Lutheran refugees with a focus on pastors and theological students.[15] Long had received an "urgent letter" from Piper recommending that Leo could be employed to minister to the German refugee community.[16] Long's office assisted in the travel arrangements and welcome to New York, although the ministry to refugees never developed. Leo and his daughter Anna became two of the first refugees given assistance by an organization that eventually became part of Lutheran Immigration and Refugee Service.

Through the mediation of Piper, Leo also attained a teaching position at Western Theological Seminary in Pittsburgh, Pennsylvania. His original teaching responsibilities were in the discipline of church history, where he was to represent a professor who had health problems. Upon receiving this employment, Leo was able to obtain US visas for himself and his daughter. Due to the many complications of beginning life in a new country, the decision was made that Anne would remain for a time with the Piper family, who also had taken in and were caring for several Jewish children.

Besides all the major adjustments involved in beginning life in a new country and culture, Leo faced two challenges in his teaching. First, he had to provide instruction in English, a language he only had learned in school. Second, he was called upon to teach church history, including American church history, a subject where his previous knowledge was minimal. Nevertheless, his students received him warmly. Dittrich noted that "with an innate humility and a redeeming sense of humor, he was liked and respected immediately."[17]

At the end of his first academic year, Leo traveled to visit his brother Ulrich, now living with his family in Venezuela. He had been writing letters regularly to Dittrich all these months, reporting his observations about the different customs and climate in the United States, and with little trace of homesickness or sentimentality

15. Solberg, *Open Doors*, 16.

16. Solberg, *Open Doors*, 17.

17. For this and the following, see Leo, "Autobiographical Notes," 11.

for having left Germany. He had also been sending monthly checks in the amount of $50 to assist with her expenses. While Dittrich lived those months with Ulrich's family, she also had been able to make connections with the local artist community. Leo arrived by plane to LaGuyra on June 30 for his visit, and his intention to marry Dittrich became immediately clear. Paul Friedrich Leo and Eva Johanna Dittrich were married in a Presbyterian chapel on July 6, 1940, at Caracas, Venezuela. All previous uncertainties were resolved. Leo's return to the United States, which originally needed to happen before July 19, was able to be extended to July 30. It was unlikely, however, that Eva's papers could be put in order in time for her to travel with her new husband under a US visa.

On the day that Paul was scheduled to depart without Eva by ocean liner to the United States, the captain of the ship refused to allow him to board because of his German nationality. Fortunately, Eva's documents arrived shortly thereafter, and they were able to depart together on a different ship, the *Maua*, on August 5. Upon arrival in New York, a colleague Paul had met in the concentration camp, Paul Peltason, arranged for them to stay at the YMCA and YWCA, respectively. In New York, they became acquainted with Central Park and the zoo. Eva, as Paul's wife, was also able to apply for her US documents. In the meantime, Paul received the distressing news that he was no longer needed in his teaching position in Pittsburgh, due to the recovery of the professor that he had been replacing. However, the seminary then offered Paul an opportunity to teach courses on biblical languages and New Testament for a salary of $50 per month and the use of a small apartment in seminary housing that was set aside for visiting missionaries.

On the trip back to Pittsburgh, Paul and Eva stopped for a few days in Princeton to visit the Piper family and Paul's daughter, Anne. At the insistence of Mrs. Piper, the decision was made to give both Anne and the new couple time to familiarize themselves with their new circumstances before Anne would join them. The apartment in Pittsburgh turned out to be very small—only a living room, small bedroom, kitchen with a dining corner, and bathroom—however, the other occupants of the house at 435 Ridge

Avenue were most gracious. The Leos became especially close to William Orr, Mildred, his wife, and their daughter, Louise, who lived on the first floor. Dr. Orr taught New Testament at Western Theological Seminary. From the Orr family, they learned more about "the American way of life" and were able to develop further their conversational English skills. News from Germany was bleak. While most family members remained alive, Paul's nephew had died as well as some of their friends.

Despite the circumstances, there was much to enjoy about life in Pittsburgh, including relationships with students and the beauty of the city. Favorite destinations included Riverside Park and the views of the Monongahela and Allegheny Rivers from Mt. Washington. The confluence of these rivers with the Ohio River was most impressive and memorable. Birthdays were celebrated with candles, flowers, and homemade gifts. Each year on June 1, they also remembered the anniversary of their first meeting at the church art exhibition in Hanover. In 1940 Christmas included special gifts and a tree with real candles. Anne visited that Christmas and enjoyed the time together.

On July 30, 1941, at 9 pm, a son was born to the Leos at Magee Hospital and named Christopher Peregrinus. This birth occasioned deep happiness but also reminded the couple of all those left behind in Germany. The name "Peregrinus" marked their wandering existence as exiles. Anne joined the family in Pittsburgh at Christmas 1941 and received the bedroom as her own space. The rest of the family shared the living room, where the crib also was located. Occasionally, Paul slept in his study at the seminary dormitory. Anne adjusted well to life and school in Pittsburgh. The family enjoyed their times reading books together.

During the years in Pittsburgh, Paul was frequently invited to speak in local church organizations about his experiences of the church struggle in Germany under Hitler. While many had succumbed to the lure of National Socialism, including pastors and theologians, a Confessing Church in resistance still persevered. Eva wrote:

> Hitler wanted to change the church into a propaganda institution for Nazi ideology, thus the church had to struggle to keep its message pure. Quite a number of theologians—professors as well as pastors—fell for Hitler partly or completely. There were even some pastors who took the cross from the altar, substituting it with a picture of Hitler. The cross had been from the beginning of the Christian church a stumbling block and a sign of rejection. There also were some pastors who defamed people of their parish at the local Nazi's headquarters because they were opponents of Hitler.[18]

Julius Bodensieck described the years from 1939 to 1943 in this summary: "Dr. Leo was quite happy as a teacher in Pittsburgh and always remembered with gratitude that the Presbyterian Church had given him asylum at the time of great need; but he knew that his place was really in the ministry of the Lutheran Church."[19] Serving Lutheran congregations in Texas became the family's next life station.

Pastoral Ministry in Texas

From 1943 to 1949 Leo served as a parish pastor for rural congregations in southern Texas. Bodensieck observed: "A fortunate combination of circumstances brought it about that a congregation in Texas belonging to the American Lutheran Church called him to be its pastor."[20] The first congregation was at Karnes City, southeast of San Antonio, where he served briefly until 1944 and the second parish was at Cave Creek and Crabapple, in the vicinity of Fredericksburg.[21] Both pastoral calls were within the Texas Synod, which had historic connections to the Iowa Synod since

18. Leo, "Autobiographical Notes," 16.

19. Bodensieck, "His Times Were in God's Hands," 10–11.

20. Julius Bodensieck, "Paul Leo," Memorial Address delivered in the Loehe Chapel of Wartburg Theological Seminary, February 13, 1958.

21. For an account of the time in Texas and a source for the following references, see Simon, "Ausgegrenzt," 99–100.

1896. Many of the members were familiar with the German language, so this provided a common bond.

Eva reported on the difficult conditions faced by the family in this unfamiliar context.[22] The little church, consisting of about 150 people, had both a church building and parsonage on an acreage that also included the parish cemetery. The area was populated by livestock and an amazing assortment of wild animals, including armadillos, skunk, opossum, snakes, lizards, and exotic birds. The family was largely left to navigate the environment by themselves, living one and a half miles from the nearest neighbors. The church buildings had been constructed by the farmers themselves at a great sacrifice of their own limited resources. The house was furnished with electrical service, a bathroom, and a telephone. The water was drawn from a well (constructed by church members), which was fed by springs and piped to the house by a wind-powered pump. It was expected that the family would tend farm animals to make living expenses more manageable for the congregation.

Pastor Paul Leo, Texas

In the second parish, Pastor Leo also served as pastor for another, somewhat smaller congregation that had its church

22. For the following, see Eva Leo, "Pfarrleben in Texas," *Neue Schau* (1955).

building twenty-five miles away. Every other Sunday, a worship service was held there, and the family also came along to spend the day. Eva described how they would need to get up at five o'clock in the morning and set out in their old automobile.[23] The road was rough with holes and deep furrows. The landscape was notable for its cornfields and pastureland with cactus and mesquite trees. When the creeks were swollen with rain, they were difficult to cross. Along the route, they met no other travelers except for occasional sightings of goat herds or deer. The family spent the entire Sunday in activities with this congregation. The return trip home was complicated by nightfall, the constellations as their traveling companions while the children slept. It was always a relief to make it home safely.

For the seventy farm families in the congregation, their church served as a culture center. They cared well for the buildings, and worship services were well attended. The hard lifestyle took its toll on all the people who lived there. In some respects, the pastor was understood as their servant, whom they had called and supported financially. It was expected that both the pastor and his wife would join in their lives and community. In addition to serving as the pastor who was responsible for the ministry of the Word, he also acted as teacher, judge in neighborly disputes, and friend. These roles, however, inevitably entailed his also becoming the object of their criticism and gossip.

Pastor Leo was not your normal country pastor—he spoke seven languages and had a Doctorate in Theology—but he never had driven a car, fixed a toilet, tightened the hinges on a door, or even mowed a lawn.[24] By contrast, Eva was a metal sculptor and a German country girl. She could grow vegetables, chop firewood, and fix a door as well as she could hammer her metalwork. Because she had no tools to work metal and no clients interested in spending money on art, she tended the never-ending daily chores

23. Eva Leo, "Pfarrleben in Texas," *Neue Schau* (1955).

24. This paragraph is adapted from Monica Leo, "Finding Home" (unpublished script, https://owlglass.org/shows/finding-home/), the script from a puppet show based on the life of the Leo family.

of a country pastor's wife. In her few spare moments, she drew pictures and water colored her life.

The parish had definite expectations for the pastor's wife, who was to teach Sunday school, work with the women's group, and participate in youth activities. Occasionally, she was asked to assist in leading the Sunday School worship service. Many members expected her to come along on pastoral visits, which could involve care for the sick and dying, or even welcoming a child at birth. Moreover, the pastor's wife served as custodian and altar guild, cleaning the church building on Saturday and preparing the altar for worship. A third child, daughter Monica, was born on October 28, 1944, during the years in Texas.

Eva, Paul, and Monica Leo (1945)

Because of his academic gifts, Dr. Leo began to be invited to deliver papers at pastoral conferences. He also was invited to lecture on three occasions at the Luther Academy, held at Wartburg Theological Seminary in Dubuque, Iowa, where he made a favorable impression on Professor J. Michael Reu, director of the academy. These connections led the Leo family to their next life station in Iowa. Despite many difficult life circumstances, Pastor Leo remembered fondly his pastoral service in Texas: "Whenever he spoke . . . about his work in Texas, his voice and his eyes indicated deep attachment to the people whom he had served."[25]

Dubuque, Iowa

When a teaching position became open in 1950 at Wartburg Theological Seminary after the resignation of President Julius Bodensieck, who was leaving for an international appointment with the US Committee of the Lutheran World Federation, Dr. Leo was invited to join the faculty as instructor in New Testament theology. This temporary position lasted for twenty months until the Board of Regents unanimously elected him to a full professorship on November 8, 1951. The promise of stability relieved the anxieties of the family about their future status.

Paul Leo Teaching in Fritschel Hall

25. Julius Bodensieck, "Paul Leo," Memorial Address delivered in the Loehe Chapel of Wartburg Theological Seminary, February 13, 1958.

The recommendation letter to the Board of Regents by Professor Samuel F. Salzmann nominating Leo for the professorship included the following qualifications:

1. Dr. Leo is a first-class scholar in the field of New Testament. He has studied under some of the most outstanding theologians of our day, and has been trained with genuine German thoroughness.

2. Dr. Leo has outstanding abilities as a teacher. He has for years served as a pastor. This gives him the pastor's view of preparing men for the ministry. He has learned to express himself simply, concretely, intelligibly. As a pastor he has served as chaplain in hospitals and penal institutions. He has knowledge of the modern science of psychiatry, and has acquired deep insights into human nature and personality. These qualities enable Dr. Leo to serve his students as a sympathetic friend and as a wise and understanding guide.

3. Dr. Leo is a conservative Lutheran by conviction. Grown up in the traditions of German theological liberalism, Dr. Leo has fought and found his way through to the evangelical faith and the sound New Testament theology of genuine Lutheranism.

4. Dr. Leo has proved himself to be an active and cooperative member of the faculty. He accepts his assignments with alacrity and thoroughness. And he has no trace of the spirit of a prima donna which might make a member of the faculty a source of irritation and disturbance among the members of the faculty and among the students.

5. Finally, Dr. Leo has an open and receptive mind to our American way of life. He loves America. He loves our American Lutheran Church. He is cultivating a remarkably effective English style. He is constantly improving himself in English speech.[26]

26. Excerpts from recommendation letter by Samuel F. Salzmann to the Board of Regents of Wartburg Seminary, Rev. Albert Heidmann, Secretary, August 23, 1951, Wartburg Theological Seminary Archives.

In his recommendation letter, Salzmann also referred to Leo's teaching effectiveness, reinforced by his overseeing students in independent study and advising an increasing number of Bachelor of Divinity theses. Salzmann also noted Leo's teaching activities in service of the church, his "timely, vital, attention-arresting and evangelical" sermons in chapel, his active membership in the local congregation of Holy Trinity Lutheran Church, and the contributions of the entire family to the seminary community.

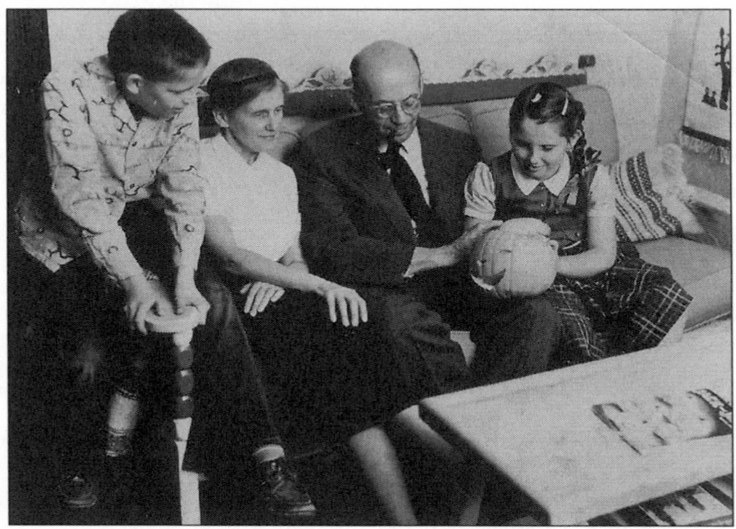

Leo Family (1955)

The Leo family in Dubuque faced new challenges and opportunities. In contrast to the years in Pittsburgh and Texas, the family was afforded better economic circumstances, especially after Paul was granted a permanent position on the faculty at Wartburg Theological Seminary. There remained many challenges, however, as the family and children were often treated as "outsiders" in the local community and schools. Discrimination against those from Germany—even those who had been forced into exile—persisted well after the end of World War II. Despite the challenges, the family managed to prosper in Iowa and the children became sufficiently well-educated to achieve their life goals. Each of the parents became citizens of the US during these years. Eva eventually developed new opportunities for her artistic work in Dubuque.

Eva and Paul Leo

Leo was recognized for many contributions to the Wartburg Seminary community, including "an unusually fruitful and richly blessed career as a teacher."

> A never-failing gentleness and patience, an almost limitless faith in the essential goodness of the students combined with a marvelous insight into the real meaning and intention of the text, a never-ceasing endeavor to penetrate even more deeply into the thinking of the New Testament writers, and an abiding faith in the Word of God as the one and only source of true knowledge of God and of salvation—all these factors make

> him an ideal teacher of New Testament interpretation in our seminary.
>
> There was no sham about Dr. Leo, no counterfeit piety, no artificiality; he was genuine and true. He disliked controversy; in fact, he was a real peacemaker. But he never concealed his convictions even if they were not popular.[27]

As an author, Leo contributed articles to the *Lutheran Quarterly* and the *Wartburg Quarterly*; these writings will be discussed in the next chapter. He had also been commissioned to write articles for the Lutheran World Encyclopedia prior to his death. Leo was both a lifelong student of the New Testament and a devoted reader of history.

Paul Leo died suddenly on Monday, February 10, 1958, while teaching a class on New Testament exegesis.[28] The prayer offered at the beginning of his final class asked God to lend a deeper appreciation and comprehension of the truth of the Gospel and for personal knowledge of the love of Jesus Christ. Students who were present in the class recalled how their professor suddenly collapsed during a discussion of the word *euangelion* (Greek for "gospel"). Paul Jersild, a student at the time, recollects:

> The day that Paul Leo died has to be indelibly marked in the memory of his students. It came totally unexpected, making it a particularly traumatic event. He was in a second floor classroom in Fritschel Hall, on a beautiful spring day in 1958, teaching one of his New Testament courses. Suddenly, without warning, he simply collapsed and died instantly.
>
> I was in the first floor classroom directly under him, and we clearly heard the thud of his body as it hit the floor. Our professor stopped his lecture and we all looked at each other, wondering what had happened. We then heard footsteps rushing to the front of the classroom, and knew something terrible had occurred.

27. Bodensieck, "His Times Were in God's Hands," 11.

28. For this and the following, see Bodensieck, "His Times Were in God's Hands," 10.

> Our class was dismissed immediately and several of us ran up the steps to the Leo classroom. It was apparent that he had died.
>
> It seemed but a few moments before students from all the classrooms had thronged into the hallway on the first floor, asking what had happened. The atmosphere quickly turned somber as the body of Professor Leo was carried by his students down the steps to the first floor. As they slowly made their way down the steps, someone began to sing "Abide with Me," and everyone began to sing. For all of us there, it had to be one of the most stirring moments of our lives, a testament to our faith and the faith of this saintly man in the midst of death.[29]

As his body was carried from the classroom in Fritschel Hall, students, staff, and faculty lined the hallways to pay their respects.

The night before he died, Leo asked his artistic wife to print a Bible text above his desk calendar: "My times are in Thy hand" (Psalm 31:15). Our days are apportioned to us by a trustworthy God, to whom we may with confidence entrust our lives. God grants us "opportunities for witnessing Christ in word and deed, amid the shifting scenes of our life, in seasons of peace and prosperity as well as in suffering and affliction."[30] From his imprisonment in Nazi Germany, forced exile, and through the life stations as an instructor in Pittsburgh, pastor in Texas, and professor in Dubuque, all his times were in God's hands.

29. Paul Jersild in a private document addressed to the author dated Nov. 20, 2017.

30. Bodensieck, "His Times Were in God's Hands," 10.

Paul Leo Grave, St. Johns Cemetery in Dubuque, Iowa

In his funeral sermon for Paul Leo based on Psalm 84, Pastor H. C. Haferman of Holy Trinity Lutheran Church proclaimed:

> There is a certain homelessness we all experience. Words such as pilgrim, sojourner, stranger, characterize our stay on earth. It is natural, then, that there should be yearning in our lives, yearning and quest for home, destination, security.[31]

These words aptly describe the sojourn of Paul Leo depicted in these biographical chapters. The book concludes with attention to Leo's teaching and scholarship in the United States.

31. Pastor H. C. Haferman, Funeral Sermon in Loehe Chapel, Wartburg Theological Seminary, February 13, 1958, Region 5/Wartburg Theological Seminary Archives.

Leo Doors in Fritschel Hall, Wartburg Theological Seminary

3

Teaching Career and Scholarship

Paul Leo served as a teaching theologian at each of his life stations in the United States. This chapter describes his teaching and scholarship from the years at Western Theological Seminary in Pittsburgh, through his service as a pastor in Texas, and to his career as a professor at Wartburg Theological Seminary in Dubuque. From this survey of his course offerings and review of his writings, we gain original perspective on Leo's theological commitments.

Prior to Leo's arrival in the United States in 1939, he had completed his Doctorate in Theology at the University of Marburg in 1928. As was typical in German theological education, he studied at several universities, focusing on history at the University of Göttingen and subsequently on theology at Tübingen and Marburg. Among his notable teachers were Rudolf Otto, Rudolf Bultmann, Karl Heim, and Adolf Schlatter. Leo wrote his dissertation on the ancient church father and monastic bishop, Basil of Caesarea.[1] His years of study were lengthened due to illness. During this time, he also wrote articles for the emerging ecumenical movement and sought to address people who had become estranged from the church.

A commentary by Leo on 1 Timothy was published in 1935 as part of the series, *Die urchristliche Botschaft: Eine Einführung in the Schriften des Neuen Testaments.* At that time Leo was serving

1. For this and the following, "Paul Leo: The Advocate."

as pastor in Osnabrück and was listed in the volume as one of the contributing editors to the series, which was under the direction of Prof. Otto Schmiz at Münster University. The commentary was entitled, *Das anvertraute Gut: Eine Einführung in den ersten Timotheusbrief*.[2] Leo stresses the unique character of the pastoral epistles within the Pauline corpus. The structure of the commentary is a straightforward discussion of 1 Timothy by chapter and verse. The title indicates the overall direction of Leo's interpretation of "The Entrusted Inheritance" (*Das anvertraute Gut*):

> The "Pastoral Epistles" make an impression of their entirely own kind among the Pauline letters. They deal with the preservation of an "entrusted inheritance," the pure and uncorrupted teaching of the faith, in view of the powers threatening the truth. What should a Christian be doing in the world as time goes on? What really is the church in this world and what is its responsibility? What is the correct way to order the congregation and to think about ecclesial offices? 1 Timothy addresses these questions, which today press upon us with urgency.[3]

Even today one can hear in these lines an echo of the German church struggle from the 1930s.

Teaching Career: Pittsburgh and Dubuque

At Western Theological Seminary in Pittsburgh, the seminary catalogs in the years from 1939 to 1943 document his teaching activities. His original appointment, which lasted for one year, was as guest professor of church history in 1939–40. That academic year Leo taught two courses, "Ecclesiastical History and History of Doctrine" and "History of Modern Theology." In this work Leo faced two major challenges: teaching subjects beyond

2. The copy of this book in the Reu Memorial Library at Wartburg Theological Seminary is inscribed by Paul Leo to J. Michael Reu at the Luther Academy held in 1947 and was from Reu's personal library.

3. Leo, *Das anvertraute Gut*, front cover.

his area of specialization in New Testament and providing instruction in the English language.

For the academic years in 1940–41, 1941–42, and 1942–43, Leo's appointment was as guest instructor in New Testament. In each of these years he taught courses in "Elementary Greek" and "The Pastoral Epistles (I, II Timothy, Titus)." The course on the Pastoral Epistles gave opportunity to teach his area of specialization and were related to the topic of his book. For the academic years in 1941–42 and 1942–43, Leo added two additional courses on "Elementary German" and "Advanced German for Students of Theology."

The Western Theological Seminary publication, *Western Towers*, included a brief biographical introduction to Dr. Leo in 1942 and in 1943 offered this description of his involvements:

> Dr. Leo bears a heavy load of teaching and private tutoring. He has preached in many churches and has delivered many addresses. He shows special insight into the European situation and has endeared himself to audiences in all parts of Western Pennsylvania.[4]

He later wrote of his time at Western Theological Seminary that he "had been treated with unforgettable graciousness, and close friendships, formed at that time, are still alive."[5]

Dr. Leo first taught at Wartburg Theological Seminary as a guest instructor for the Luther Academy in 1948, when his topic was "Studies in the Letter to the Hebrews." Working from a detailed outline of the entire letter, Leo commented on the author, audience, and context of the epistle as his approach to teaching Hebrews. The three main sections of his outline were: (1) The Old and New Covenant, (2) Christ the Great High Priest and His Work, and (3) The Answer of Man: Faith. Leo emphasized the uniqueness of Christ's priesthood and Christ's sacrifice. The

4. *Western Towers*, February 1943 issue, published by Western Theological Seminary, Pittsburgh, Pennsylvania, 35. Paul Leo is also included in a photo of the entire faculty on 36.

5. Leo, "Meaning of New Testament Exegesis," 3.

proper response by human beings was to answer in faith as had the generations before us.[6]

Leo taught at the Luther Academy on at least two other occasions. In 1951 his topic was "The Meaning of New Testament Exegesis." Leo offered these introductory words:

> As I try to give expression to my feelings in this hour, what is uppermost in my heart is consciousness of the sincere love for Wartburg Seminary that I felt from the moment when I was its guest for the first time. It was exactly ten years ago, and I was still a babe in this country, when I received the invitation from the sainted Dr. Reu to give some lectures at that summer's Luther Academy. And at that Academy for the first time I felt completely at home since I came to this country.[7]

In 1955 the topic was "Revelation and History: A Study of the Theology of J. C. K. von Hofmann." These reflections bear witness to Leo's finding his place within the Wartburg Theological Seminary community. The latter presentation on Hofmann was divided into two parts: (1) The Man and His Work, and (2) His Significance for Our Time. Both presentations resulted in publications, which will be discussed in the next section.

During these years, Wartburg Theological Seminary held an annual event called Founders' Day. On two occasions Leo served as lecturer: once prior to joining the faculty and once during his tenure on the faculty. In 1948 Leo presented on the topic, "Melchizedek and Christ," which accords with his teaching at the Luther Academy earlier that year. In 1956 Leo delivered the address, "The Divinity of the Call," as one of the Reu Memorial Lectures held November 1–2. Both addresses are discussed among his publications.

The teaching career of Paul Leo on the faculty of Wartburg Theological Seminary began with his appointment as instructor of

6. An outline of Paul Leo's presentation on Hebrews, dated July 21, 1948, Region 5 Archives for the Evangelical Lutheran Church in America and the Wartburg Theological Seminary Archives.

7. Leo, "Meaning of New Testament Exegesis," 3.

New Testament in the Department of Exegetical Theology for the 1950–51 and 1951–52 academic years. His teaching schedule, according to the seminary catalog, was the same for both years. During each of these four semesters, he taught the following courses: New Testament Introduction, New Testament Exegesis, and New Testament Seminar. During the two fall semesters, he also taught Reading in the Greek New Testament, and in spring semesters, he taught a continuation of New Testament Exegesis.

Upon his election as professor of New Testament in the Department of Exegetical Theology, Leo taught the following courses in the 1952–53, 1953–54, 1954–55, and 1955–56 academic years: Reading in the Greek New Testament (fall), New Testament Introduction (spring), New Testament Exegesis (two-course sequence, fall and spring), and New Testament Seminar (two-course sequence, fall and spring). In the 1956–57 and 1957–58 academic years he offered: New Testament Exegesis (two-course sequence, fall and spring), Exegesis on Basis of the English Bible (spring), New Testament Introduction (spring), and New Testament Seminar (two-course sequence, fall and spring).

Professor Leo clearly specialized in the exegesis and interpretation of the New Testament in his teaching at Wartburg Theological Seminary. The offering of the new course, Exegesis on the Basis of the English Bible, was an innovation at a seminary committed to interpretation based on the original biblical languages. During these years, Leo's colleagues in the Department of Exegetical Theology included August J. Engelbrecht and Ethan Mengers (who joined the faculty in 1956–57 when Trinity Seminary at Blair, Nebraska, merged with Wartburg Seminary). Julius H. Bodensieck was listed as an alternate teacher for some of the courses offered in 1955–56 and 1957–58. Gerhard Krodel became Leo's successor in 1958–59.

Publications

During his years at Western Theological Seminary, Leo published the article, "The Bearing of the German Church Struggle on

Theology," in the *Journal of Theology of the American Lutheran Conference*.[8] This is the earliest publication by Leo in the US and provides his interpretation of the resistance of the Confessing Church against the false teachings of National Socialism. Leo began by describing the necessary task of clarifying the core doctrine of the church in contradistinction to the distortions of the German Christians. In every era of conflict, the church has needed to return to its confessional foundations, even drafting new creeds. The church struggle provided the occasion for formulating new statements of faith to provide solid groundwork in this time of crisis.[9] Creeds originated as "answers to some definite challenge, always weapons of defense against some specific attack."[10] They reoriented the church to Scripture and, in the case of the Reformers, to the teachings of the Confessions. Leo highlighted the Barmen Declaration of 1934 as of singular significance for building common theological ground.[11]

The anti-Semitism of the Nazi program contradicted the Jewish origins of both Judaism and Christianity: "a willingness to antagonize the Jewish spirit within the Bible and try to cleanse the Bible of its Jewish ingredients."[12] National Socialism sought to coerce the church by incorporating church governance into the state apparatus, which Leo details from contemporary events. He cites with appreciation the leadership of the Confessing Church by Karl Barth and Martin Niemöller in countering racialism in church and society through their clear focus on Jesus Christ as the Word of God who overcomes all divisions. While writing objectively, we know how much Leo himself was affected by the policies of the government: "As to the non-Aryan ministers, resistance to

8. Leo, "Bearing of the German Church Struggle," 102–15.

9. See the documentation of the church struggle for right confession in the 3 volumes assembled by Schmidt, *Die Bekenntnisse*.

10. Leo, "Bearing of the German Church Struggle," 105.

11. The Theological Declaration of Barmen, https://www.ekd.de/en/The-Barmen-Declaration-303.htm.

12. Leo, "Bearing of the German Church Struggle," 108.

the government became more and more impracticable; the church was *forced* to remove them one by one."[13]

The proclivity, especially of the Lutheran church, toward obedience to the state complicated its capacity to respond to the political situation. With prescience, Leo commented "that we are now living in the time of the decline of this Constantinian era in the Church."[14] He concludes by noting that while his experience in the US has been limited, here too there exists a race problem that can only be addressed "by the absolute validity of the Bible as God's revelation and the absolute power of Christ as the Lord of the Church."[15] It is valuable to have this record of Leo's witness to the German church struggle as documentation of the presentations he made on this theme during his years in Pittsburgh.

Six essays by Leo appeared as publications between 1948 and 1958 in relation to his teaching and professorship at Wartburg Theological Seminary. The first two were prior to his joining the seminary faculty, and the final one was in the year of his death. Each of these will be briefly summarized and discussed in the order of their appearance.

The earliest of these publications by Paul Leo appeared in the *Wartburg Seminary Quarterly* in December 1948 and was thematically related to his lectures on the Letter to the Hebrews at the Luther Academy earlier that year.[16] His specific focus was on Melchizedek in Hebrews 7:1–10, which is instructive for biblical interpretation in relating the Old and New Testaments. Melchizedek is introduced as a forerunner of the Messiah, "the priestly king who points toward Christ."[17] Leo attended first to the meaning of the name, Melchizedek, king of Salem. Melchizedek literally means "king of righteousness" and Salem means "peace," both being characteristics of the messianic rule anticipated by the prophets. The meeting of Melchizedek with Abraham gave him

13. Leo, "Bearing of the German Church Struggle," 112.
14. Leo, "Bearing of the German Church Struggle," 114.
15. Leo, "Bearing of the German Church Struggle," 115.
16. Leo, "Melchizedek and Christ," 3–9.
17. Leo, "Melchizedek and Christ," 3.

significance for the history of salvation. Leo discounted speculative interpretations that sought to go beyond the biblical text. Because nothing is recorded about the beginning or end of his priesthood, Melchizedek "points forward to Christ."[18] By blessing Abraham, Melchizedek was blessing his seed who is Christ. Leo underscored the scriptural (contrasted with "radical historical criticism") and christological ("prophetic") character of this text from Hebrews, the inauguration of Christ's new priesthood.[19]

The second publication appeared in the June 1949 issue of the *Wartburg Seminary Quarterly* and was also based on his Luther Academy lectures on Hebrews. This article was based on Hebrews 11–12 and was entitled "The Believer's Lineage."

> We may call the Epistle to the Hebrews an ellipse with two foci: Christ on the one side, man's answer through faith on the other. We may go further and say that the whole presentation of God's act has the purpose of encouraging man to give his answer—it is the intention of the letter to strengthen faith.[20]

These pivotal chapters encouraged readers of the letter to be sustained by the great cloud of witnesses who lived by faith as "the assurance of things hoped for" (Heb 11:1). The message is not intended for an audience of new Christians but rather as encouragement to those in danger of losing their faith. Leo interpreted the named biblical witnesses as "the lineage of believers," whom God encouraged to remain faithful in their own circumstances and who now provide solace and solidarity as we in our own time run the race set before us. In this article Leo draws exegetical insights and makes references to contemporary scholars, such as Adolf Schlatter. "In Hebrews faith is closely related to patience, endurance, steadfastness, courage. We are shown faith is not an easy thing. We

18. Leo, "Melchizedek and Christ," 5.

19. Leo, "Melchizedek and Christ," 7–8.

20. Leo, "Believer's Lineage," 5.

do not receive it and then sit down and relax."[21] Leo stressed that the "only and exclusive way to God is faith."[22]

The third publication was based on his presentation at the Luther Academy in July 1952 and was entitled "The Meaning of New Testament Exegesis." In this article Leo, now teaching New Testament exegesis at the seminary on a regular basis, reflected on methodological issues. He approached the text under the presupposition that in the Bible God's own revelation has been disclosed in both Old and New Testament. Exegesis, therefore, is a single discipline with which the interrelationship of both testaments deserves attention. Leo followed Luther in holding that the New Testament is "the poor swaddling clothes into which the Christ child has been laid," which by its very nature has both "a truly human and truly divine aspect."[23] The Bible reflects the finite condition of humanity, bound to the languages in which they were written. This means, as with Luther, it is imperative to engage the interpretation of Scripture in the original biblical languages. Only so can we begin to grasp the subtleties and significance of the text, grounded in their historical contexts and influenced primarily by the Jewish world but also by Hellenistic philosophy.

The exegete must understand literary style in accordance with textual origins. Each step of the exegetical process serves as preliminary work for delivering to contemporary hearers a message that comes alive as the Word of God. Leo warned against the dangers of rationalism, dogmatism, and subjectivism in relation to the nineteenth- and twentieth-century theological discussions, making reference to several scholars, including Rudolf Bultmann and Karl Barth. In conclusion, he shares this conviction: "Every pastor must be able to do sound exegetical work. Therefore it must be learned in the seminary, but always with the outlook toward, and a living contact with, the life of the congregation."[24] We see here Leo's key role in the educational process for ministry practitioners.

21. Leo, "Believer's Lineage," 11.

22. Leo, "Believer's Lineage," 12.

23. Leo, "Meaning of New Testament Exegesis," 4.

24. Leo, "Meaning of New Testament Exegesis," 10.

The fourth publication takes up one of the most controversial figures in the New Testament research of Leo's time and is entitled, "Kerygma and Mythos: The Theology of Rudolf Bultmann."[25] Leo is thoroughly conversant with Bultmann's writings and accurately summarized them in relation to contemporary New Testament research in the first sections of the essay. He argued that Bultmann should be viewed neither as a representative of liberalism nor as a radical historical critic. Bultmann's program involves preserving the New Testament *kerygma* through a process of reinterpreting the mythological worldview in order to reclaim and reinterpret the Christian message. Leo sought to clarify what Bultmann meant by mythology against unwarranted criticisms. He describes how Bultmann employed existentialist categories to communicate the truth claims of the New Testament in contemporary language. This means placing the "Christ-event" at the heart of the matter, which involves preserving the cross-resurrection event of Jesus Christ as decisive for human existence. This occurs through our proclamation of Christ as God's saving event to be received in faith.

Leo sought to encourage readers not to be reactive about the provocative aspects of Bultmann's work, but instead to recognize his intellectual honesty and faithful intent. His own chief criticism involved how Bultmann shifts the center of gravity in the New Testament away from the resurrection to the faith of the disciples:

> As far as the life of Christ is concerned, it simply takes the heart out of the New Testament message if we regard not the resurrection, but the faith of the disciples in the resurrection as the basic fact which constitutes the church. We fully agree with Barth that the truth that the Word became flesh in Jesus Christ, and not the *kerygma* of this truth must be accepted as the center of the biblical message. We cannot give up the conviction that a real *Heilsgeschichte* is the heart of the Bible.[26]

It is bracing to see the deep engagement of Leo with the theology of Bultmann, one of the most controversial figures of the time.

25. Leo, "Kerygma and Mythos," 359–70.

26. Leo, "Kerygma and Mythos," 369.

The fifth publication originated as a lecture delivered by Leo to a pastor's conference in Aberdeen, South Dakota, and is titled "The Divinity of the Call." By way of definition, Leo contrasted a "direct call," which is one that comes immediately from God, to an "indirect call," which is mediated through another person or group, such as a congregation. Both provide instances of "external call"—a call that comes from beyond oneself. By comparison, an "internal call" arises from an inner conviction—either through gradual or sudden insight—that one is being compelled by God to a certain form of service. In this way, an internal call is intimately connected to one's personal experience. With reference to the Lutheran Confessions, Leo specifies that the charge to proclaim the Gospel and administer the sacraments is discharged by "divine right."[27] By contrast, the church establishes other ordinances by "human right," for example, the church's expectations about how to prepare leaders for the ministry of Word and Sacrament. In negotiating terms of employment, pastoral ministry should not be understood as a holier calling but rather analogous to other types of work. Finally, Leo cites Sigmund Fritschel and the theologians of the Iowa Synod in distinguishing between the divine institution of the ministry of Word and Sacrament and the human ecclesiastical ordinances that regulate the exercise of that office.[28]

The sixth and most extensive publication by Leo deals with a topic he had earlier taken up at the Luther Academy in 1955 under the title, "Revelation and History in J. C. K. von Hofmann."[29] Published posthumously, this article demonstrates Leo's engagement with contemporary themes in biblical hermeneutics, as did his previous writing for *Lutheran Quarterly.* Although Hofmann was a nineteenth-century theologian, Leo contended that his thought continues to have implications for recent discussion of issues relating revelation and history. After a careful review of Hofmann's substantive contributions to the development of salvation history (*Heilsgeschichte*), Leo noted how Hofmann organized his

27. Leo, "Divinity of the Call," 7.

28. Leo, "Divinity of the Call," 11.

29. Leo, "Revelation and History," 195–216.

thought to encompass both unity and variety in Scripture. While he acknowledges how some of Hoffman's exegetical conclusions are no longer accurate, Leo also asserts that methodologically Hofmann developed a typology of "prophecy and fulfillment," which has been taken up by recent biblical and systematic theologians.[30] Hofmann proved fruitful as a theologian who understood how the believer's experience of God is mediated through education, preaching, and Scripture study.

Leo names three areas of disagreement with Hofmann, each related to the influence of nineteenth-century philosophy on his thought: his overemphasis on individual religious experience, his tendency toward speculation and rationalization rather than centering on divine revelation in biblical history, and his failure adequately to claim the Word of God as the material substance for theological thinking.[31]

> The Bible is not only an historical report; it also is the *living Word*. This Word not only reports; it addresses us directly. We are not only objective spectators; we are involved. It shows us our inner life. It opens our eyes to our sin and disobedience, to the fact that we are living our life apart from God. It brings us the personal, comforting message that Christ has come to me and to you to open for us the way to God and to heaven.[32]

Despite these criticisms, Leo commended the usefulness of Hofmann's writings for biblical interpretation, especially for demonstrating the principle of *analogia fidei*. "The greatness of Hofmann's teaching lies in his insight into the theological unity of the Bible which appears in the form of historical variety."[33] As

30. Leo, "Revelation and History," 201–5.

31. Leo, "Revelation and History," 206–9.

32. Leo, "Revelation and History," 212. At the Centenary of Wartburg Theological Seminary, Samuel F. Salzmann placed comparable stress on the theology of Wartburg Seminary as a "theology of the Word." See Salzmann, "Theology of Wartburg Seminary," 11–23. One notes the similarity of Leo's convictions articulated here.

33. Leo, "Revelation and History," 215.

in his earlier writing, he connected his topic to the contemporary theological discussion, including the provocative views of Bultmann and Gogarten.

At the time of his death, Leo had been commissioned to write several articles for the Lutheran World Encyclopedia. Leo's lively contributions to church and academy through his writings as a professor at Wartburg Theological Seminary make the grief surrounding his tragic death even more acute.

Conclusion

We conclude this overview of the teaching career and scholarship of Paul Leo with references to his final sermon and his published autobiographical remarks about finding a home at Wartburg Theological Seminary. Leo's last sermon was preached in Loehe Chapel on January 15, 1958, and was based on the following text from 2 Cor 7:8–12:

> For even if I made you sorry with my letter, I do not regret it (though I did regret it, for I see that I grieved you with that letter, though only briefly). Now I rejoice, not because you were grieved, but because your grief led to repentance; for you felt a godly grief, so that you were not harmed in any way by us. For godly grief produces a repentance that leads to salvation and brings no regret, but worldly grief produces death. For see what earnestness this godly grief has produced in you, what eagerness to clear yourselves, what indignation, what alarm, what longing, what zeal, what punishment! At every point you have proved yourselves guiltless in the matter. So although I wrote to you, it was not on account of the one who did the wrong, nor on account of the one who was wronged, but in order that your zeal for us might be made known to you before God.[34]

The sermon is a retrospective on the end of the fall semester and provides a glimpse into what Pastor Leo valued as he counseled

34. Region 5/Wartburg Theological Seminary Archives.

others about looking at the past. He posed probing questions to the seminary community, such as: "What are the things in our life that we really ought to regret? What are the things that should cause us grief as we are looking back to them?"[35]

Leo's focus is very precise. He invited reflection about those things that were fully within our control, yet were also where we failed—including the ways we fail each other in the academic community. At the heart of the sermon Leo accents the distinction between "worldly grief" and "godly grief."

> For godly grief produces a repentance that leads to salvation and brings no regret, but worldly grief produces death.[36]

Worldly grief is characterized by selfishness and generates feelings of anger and bitterness. Worldly grief cannot bear the burden of genuine honesty and sincerity. Worldly grief aspires to be esteemed by others rather than living in humility. In contrast, the Apostle Paul commended "Godlike grief" to the Corinthian congregation.[37] Godly grief admits that the self is alienated from God's will and in need of repentance. Out of the pain caused by admonition, Christians are summoned to enter "prayerful self-examination." We are called to turn from the opinions of others and to pay sole attention to the judgment of God. In the words of Hebrews 4:12, the Word of God pierces "the division of soul and spirit" to lay us bare in God's presence.

Only godly grief leads to eternal life and can serve as the source for a new beginning.[38] Repentance is "never merely sadness, it is always the beginning of joy." Through such godly grief, we are prepared by God for the Holy Communion that can "renew the friendship between us as members of this seminary."

> Let us not live together in that superficial type of friendship, which deserves not the name of Christian

35. Leo, "Chapel Service," 1.

36. Leo, "Chapel Service," 1.

37. Leo, "Chapel Service," 2–3.

38. For this and the following quote, Leo, "Chapel Service," 4.

> friendship, in which we just get along with each other in external harmony but avoid a serious word in order to spare each other a feeling of godly grief. And on the other hand: let each one of us always be ready to listen in love to such a word of truth, even if it hurts. It might be just the word of life that we need in this moment.[39]

Reading this sermon today, we detect the forthrightness and genuine pastoral concern proclaimed by Pastor Leo, centered on his hope in the Gospel of Jesus Christ.

Exiled from Germany under unimaginable circumstances and at great personal loss, Paul Leo, as a pastor and theologian of the church, was able to maintain confidence in the providence of God. His life stations in the United States gave him remarkable opportunities to provide for his family, develop friendships, serve in Christian ministry, and share his considerable gifts as a teacher. It was a cause for deep gratitude that this journey led him to Wartburg Theological Seminary. In an uncharacteristic autobiographical reference, Leo wrote:

> But it was a great experience to be among fellow Lutherans again, to worship in the chapel that was named after Wilhelm Loehe, on the whole to breathe an air that was entirely familiar to me. When I came home I said to my wife: this was bone of my bone and flesh of my flesh. Two more times the following decade I was permitted to return to Wartburg Seminary and each time I felt: this is the place I love in my new homeland. And I do not know how to give true expression to my feelings of gratitude towards God and men for being deemed worthy to become a member of the household of this institution, and to participate in its work as a member of the family. I took my oath of installation with a deep and prayerful wish that God may help me to justify the confidence of the American Lutheran Church and especially the Board of Regents that I have been shown by calling me into this

39. Leo, "Chapel Service," 4.

> position. I feel that this is a task which cannot be fulfilled except by the constant support of the Holy Spirit.[40]

It is fitting and proper that the legacy of Paul and Eva Leo remains a cherished contribution to the history of Wartburg Theological Seminary to this day. As Julius Bodensieck wrote in his obituary: "Let us give glory and thanks to God for having placed so true and genuine a witness of Christ in our midst, and may we never forget Paul Leo's message and example. Blessed are the pure in heart: For they shall see God."[41]

40. Leo, "Meaning of New Testament Exegesis," 3.
41. Bodensieck, "His Times Were in God's Hands," 11.

Leo Doors in Loehe Chapel, Wartburg Theological Seminary

Chronology of Paul Leo (1893–1958)

January 9, 1893	Born in Göttingen, Germany
Easter 1912	Graduation from the Gymnasium in Göttingen
1912–19	Theological Study in Tübingen and Marburg
1919	Completion of First Theological Exam
1919–20	Continued Theological Study in Marburg
1921–22	Eighteen Months as Pastoral Candidate; Study at Preachers Seminary in Erichsburg
1922	Completion of Second Theological Exam
August 20, 1922	Ordination in Aurich
1922–27	Colleague and Substitute Pastor in Norderney
1927–30	Pastor in Neuhaus-Silberborn
1928	Licentiate in Theology from the University of Marburg at Completion of Doctoral Dissertation on Basil the Great
September 17, 1929	Marriage with Anna Siegert

May 9, 1931	Birth of Daughter, Anna Leo
May 18, 1931	Death of Wife, Anna Leo
1930–38	Special Counseling Position (Anstaltsgeistlicher) in Osnabrück
1938	Prisoner in Buchenwald Concentration Camp
1939	Refugee Camp in the Netherlands
1939–40	Guest Professor of Church History, Western Theological Seminary, Pittsburgh, Pennsylvania
July 6, 1940	Marriage with Eva Dittrich
July 30, 1941	Birth of Son, Christopher Peregrinus Leo
1940–43	Guest Instructor in New Testament, Western Theological Seminary
1943–45	Pastor in Karnes City, Texas
October 28, 1944	Birth of Daughter, Monica Cecilie Leo
1945–50	Pastor of St. John Lutheran Church in Crabapple and St. Paul Lutheran Church in Cave Creek, Texas
August 21, 1950	Becomes Citizen of the United States of America
1950–52	Instructor in New Testament Theology, Wartburg Theological Seminary, Dubuque, Iowa
1952–58	Professor of New Testament, Wartburg Theological Seminary
February 10, 1958	Death at Wartburg Theological Seminary, Dubuque, Iowa, USA

Sources for the Biography of Paul Leo

Becker, Heidrun. "Der Osnabrücker Kreis 1931–1939." In *Bewahren ohne Bekennen? Die hannoversche Landeskirche im Nationalsozialismus*, edited by Heinrich Grosse, Hans Otte, and Joachim Perels, 43–104. Hannover: Lutherisches Verlagshaus, 1996.

———. "Zur Rolle des Osnabrücker Kreises in der Hannoverschen Landeskirche 1931–1947." Master's Thesis, Leibniz University of Hannover, 1996.

Befeldt, Peter. "Paul Leo: Evangelischer Pastor jüdischer Herkunft." Osnabrück Student Paper. Osnabrück University, Hildesheim, 2003.

Bodensieck, Julius. "His Times Were in God's Hands." *The Lutheran Standard* 66 (March 8, 1958) 10–11.

Brandy, Hans Christian. "Gustav Oehlert und Paul Leo. Zwei Pastoren jüdischer Herkunft." In der Evangelisch-lutherischen Landeskirche Hannovers." *Jahrbuch der Gesellschaft für Niedersächsische Kirchengeschichte* 93 (1995) 193–238.

———. "Gustav Oehlert und Paul Leo. Zwei Pastoren jüdischer Herkunft in der Evangelisch-lutherischen Landeskirche Hannovers." *Bewahren ohne Bekennen? Die hannoversche Landeskirche im Nationalsozialismus*, edited by Heinrich Grosse, Hans Otte, and Joachim Perels, 375–427. Hannover: Lutherisches Verlagshaus, 1996.

Hauschild, Wolf-Dieter. "Evangelische Theologen im Exil." In *Die Künste und die Wissenschaften im Exil 1933–1945*, edited by Edith Böhne and Wolfgang Motzkau-Valeton, 257–97. Gerlingen: L. Schneider, 1992.

Leo, Eva. "Autobiographical Notes." Unpublished manuscript. Region 5/ Wartburg Theological Seminary Archives.

———. "Biographie Paul Leos." Dubuque 1960, Landeskirchliches Archiv Hannover, S1 HII 920, Nachlass Prof. Lic. Paul Leo, Dubuque (Iowa), Bl. 39–54.

———. "Pfarrleben in Texas." *Neue Schau* (1955).

Leo Ellis, Anne. "Last Stop, Prickly Pear." Unpublished Manuscript, New York, 2010.

Maßner, Joachim. "Paul Friedrich Leo." In *Biographisches Handbuch zur Geschichte der Region Osnabrück*, edited by Rainer Hehemann, 180–81. Osnabrück: Rasch, 1990.

Simon, Bettina. "Ausgegrenzt, entrechtet, verraten. Paul Leo. Biographische Spuren-suche im Kontext des Verhaltens der ev.-luth. Landeskirche Hannovers (1933ff) gegenűber ihren Pastoren jűdischer Herkunft." Qualifying Paper under the Direction of Professor Eberhard Busch, University of Göttingen, 1996.

Writings by Paul Leo

Leo, Paul. *Das anvertraute Gut: Eine Einführung in den ersten Timotheusbrief.* Berlin: Furche, 1935.

———. "The Bearing of the German Church Struggle on Theology." *Journal of Theology of the American Lutheran Conference* 7 (February 1942) 102–15.

———. "The Believer's Lineage." *Wartburg Seminary Quarterly* 12 (June 1949) 5–12.

———. "Denkschrift: Kirche und Judentum" (1933). In *Die lutherische Landeskirche Hannovers und ihr Bischof 1933–1945. Dokumente*, edited by Eberhard Klügel, 189–96. Berlin: Lutherisches Verlagshaus, 1965.

———. "The Divinity of the Call." *Wartburg Seminary Quarterly* 19 (September 1956) 4–12.

———. "Kerygma and Mythos: The Theology of Rudolf Bultmann." *Lutheran Quarterly* 5 (November 1953) 359–70.

———. "The Meaning of New Testament Exegesis." *Wartburg Seminary Quarterly* 16 (March 1952) 3–11.

———. "Melchizedek and Christ." *Wartburg Seminary Quarterly* 12 (December 1948) 3–9.

———. "Revelation and History in J. C. K. von Hofmann." *Lutheran Quarterly* 10 (August 1958) 195–216.

———. "Unsere Stellung zum Sozialismus." *Badezeitung und Anzeiger für das Nordseebad Norderney.* March 1925.

———. "Die Wirkung Basilius' des Grossen auf das Mönchtum seiner Zeit." ThD diss., Philipps-University Marburg, 1928.

———. "Die Wirkung Basilius' des Grossen auf das Mönchtum seiner Zeit." Abbreviated diss., Georg August University of Göttingen, 1929.

Photo Catalogue

In order of appearance:	Courtesy of:
1. Paul Leo (1893–1958)	Monica Leo, West Liberty, Iowa
2. Paul Leo as Youth	Monica Leo, West Liberty, Iowa
3. Title Page of Dissertation	Carsten Linden, Lemförde, Germany
4. Dismissal of Paul Leo (8/17/1935)	Archives of Kirchenkreis Osnabrück, Germany
5. Paul Leo Passport (Categorized Jew)	Monica Leo, West Liberty, Iowa
6. News Article: Jew Leo (1/22/1939)	University Library, Bremen, Germany
7. Remembrance Plaque in Norderney	Stephan Berhardt, Norderney, Germany
8. Street Sign in Osnabrück	Carsten Linden, Lemförde, Germany
9. Paul and Eva Leo Family	Monica Leo, West Liberty, Iowa

In order of appearance:	Courtesy of:
10. Passport Photo of Paul Leo (1939)	Anne Leo Ellis, New York, New York
11. Passport Photo of Anna Leo (1939)	Anne Leo Ellis, New York, New York
12. Friedrich Harjes with Eva Dittrich	Tobias Harjes, Schwanewede, Germany
13. Workshop of Friedrich Harjes	Tobias Harjes, Schwanewede, Germany
14. Pastor Paul Leo, Texas	Monica Leo, West Liberty, Iowa
15. Eva, Paul, and Monica Leo (1945)	Monica Leo, West Liberty, Iowa
16. Paul Leo Teaching in Fritschel Hall	Monica Leo, West Liberty, Iowa
17. Leo Family (1955)	Monica Leo, West Liberty, Iowa
18. Eva and Paul Leo	Monica Leo, West Liberty, Iowa
19. Paul Leo Grave, St. Johns Cemetery	Archives of Wartburg Seminary, Dubuque, Iowa
20. Leo Doors at Wartburg Seminary	Craig Nessan, Dubuque, Iowa
21. Leo Doors at Wartburg Seminary	Craig Nessan, Dubuque, Iowa

Bibliography

Andryszak, Lisa, and Christiane Bramkamp, eds. *Jüdisches Leben auf Norderney: Präsenz, Vielfalt und Ausgrenzung*. Berlin: Lit, 2014.

Becker, Heidrun. "Der Osnabrücker Kreis 1931–1939." In *Bewahren ohne Bekennen? Die hannoversche Landeskirche im Nationalsozialismus*, edited by Heinrich Grosse, Hans Otte, and Joachim Perels, 43–104. Hannover: Lutherisches Verlagshaus, 1996.

———. "Zur Rolle des Osnabrücker Kreises in der Hannoverschen Landeskirche 1931–1947." Master's Thesis, Leibniz University of Hannover, 1996.

Befeldt, Peter. "Paul Leo: Evangelischer Pastor jüdischer Herkunft." Osnabrück Student Paper. Osnabrück University, Hildesheim, 2003.

Berger, Eva. *Wer bürgt für die Kosten? 125 Jahre Stadtkrankenhaus Osnabrück. 180 Jahre städtische Gesundheitspolitik*. Osnabrück: Rasch, 1991.

Blitz, Hugo. *Evangelisch-lutherisches Gemeindebuch für Osnabrück*. Osnabrück: Meinders and Elstermann, 1927.

Bodensieck, Julius. "His Times Were in God's Hands." *The Lutheran Standard* 66 (March 8, 1958) 10–11.

Boeckler, Annette M. "Das Mutterprinzip." *Juedische Allgemeine*, April 29, 2013. https://www.juedische-allgemeine.de/religion/das-mutterprinzip/.

Brandy, Hans Christian. "Gustav Oehlert und Paul Leo. Zwei Pastoren jüdischer Herkunft in der Evangelisch-lutherischen Landeskirche Hannovers." *Jahrbuch der Gesellschaft für Niedersächsische Kirchengeschichte* 93 (1995) 193–238.

———. "Gustav Oehlert und Paul Leo. Zwei Pastoren jüdischer Herkunft in der Evangelisch-lutherischen Landeskirche Hannovers." *Bewahren ohne Bekennen? Die hannoversche Landeskirche im Nationalsozialismus*, edited by Heinrich Grosse, Hans Otte, and Joachim Perels, 375–427. Hannover: Lutherisches Verlagshaus, 1996.

Brunotte, Heinz. "Die jungevangelische Bewegung 1927–1933." *Jahrbuch der Gesellschaft für niedersächsische Kirchengeschichte* 77 (1979) 175–96.

Cohn, Werner. "Bearers of Common Fate? The 'Non-Aryan Christian Fate-Comrades' of the Paulus Bund 1933–1939." *Leo Baeck Institute Yearbook* 23 (1988) 327–66.

Drewes, Hans-Gerd. "Geschichte der öffentlichen Krankenhäuser in Osnabrück unter Berücksichtigung der chirurgischen Einrichtungen." Diss., Heinrich Heine University Düsseldorf, 1974.

Ericksen, Robert. "Luther, Lutherans and the German Church Struggle." *Kirchliche Zeitgeschichte* 1 (1999) 297–307.

"Eva Leo." Wikipedia, n.d. https://en.wikipedia.org/wiki/Eva_Leo.

Fürst, Walter, ed. *Scheidung und Bewährung 1933–1936: Aufsätze, Gutachten und Erklärungen*. Munich: Christian Kaiser, 1966.

Gartmann, Franz, and Wolfgang Reichel. "Aufstieg und Machtübernahme der NSDAP in Osnabrück." State Exam Thesis. Osnabrück University, 1975.

"German Metal Sculptor: Eva Leo." People Pill, n.d. https://peoplepill.com/i/eva-leo/.

Glufke, Dirk. "Richard Karwehls 'Politisches Messiastum. Zur Auseinandersetzung zwischen Kirche und Nationalsozialismus.'" *Jahrbuch der Gesellschaft für niedersächsische Kirchengeschichte* 90 (1992) 201–17.

Goldhagen, Daniel Jonah. *Worse Than War: Genocide, Eliminationism, and the Ongoing Assault on Humanity*. New York: Public Affairs, 2009.

Grosse, Heinrich, Hans Otte, and Joachim Perels, eds. *Bewahren ohne Bekennen? Die Hannoversche Landeskirche im Nationalsozialismus*. Hannover: Lutherisches Verlagshaus, 1996.

Hauschild, Wolf-Dieter. "Evangelische Theologen im Exil." In *Die Künste und die Wissenschaften im Exil 1933–1945*, edited by Edith Böhne and Wolfgang Motzkau-Valeton, 257–97. Gerlingen: L. Schneider, 1992.

Hehemann, Rainer. *Biographisches Handbuch zur Geschichte der Region Osnabrück*. Osnabrück: Rasch, 1990.

Hübinger, Gangolf. *Kulturprotestantismus und Politik: Zum Verhältnis von Liberalismus und Protestantismus im wilhelminischen Deutschland*. Tübingen: Mohr Siebeck, 1994.

Junk, Peter, and Martina Sellmeyer. *Stationen auf dem Weg nach Auschwitz: Entrechtung, Vertreibung, Vernichtung. Juden in Osnabrück 1900–1945*. 2nd ed. Bramsche: Rasch, 1989.

Klügel, Eberhard. *Die lutherische Landeskirche Hannovers und ihr Bischof 1933–1945. Dokumente*. Berlin: Lutherisches Verlagshaus, 1965.

Kühling, Karl. *Osnabrück 1933–1945: Stadt im Dritten Reich*. 2nd ed. Osnabrück: Wenner, 1980.

Leo, Eva. "Autobiographical Notes." Unpublished manuscript. Region 5/ Wartburg Theological Seminary Archives.

———. "Biographie Paul Leos." Dubuque 1960, Landeskirchliches Archiv Hannover, S1 HII 920, Nachlass Prof. Lic. Paul Leo, Dubuque (Iowa), Bl. 39–54.

Leo, Paul. *Das anvertraute Gut: Eine Einführung in den ersten Timotheusbrief*. Berlin: Furche, 1935.

———. "The Bearing of the German Church Struggle on Theology." *Journal of Theology of the American Lutheran Conference* 7 (February 1942) 102–15.

———. "The Believer's Lineage." *Wartburg Seminary Quarterly* 12 (June 1949) 5–12.

———. "Denkschrift: Kirche und Judentum" (1933). In *Die lutherische Landeskirche Hannovers und ihr Bischof 1933–1945. Dokumente*, edited by Eberhard Klügel, 189–96. Berlin: Lutherisches Verlagshaus, 1965.

———. "The Divinity of the Call." *Wartburg Seminary Quarterly* 19 (September 1956) 4–12.

———. "Kerygma and Mythos: The Theology of Rudolf Bultmann." *Lutheran Quarterly* 5 (November 1953) 359–70.

———. "The Meaning of New Testament Exegesis." *Wartburg Seminary Quarterly* 16 (March 1952) 3–11.

———. "Melchizedek and Christ." *Wartburg Seminary Quarterly* 12 (December 1948) 3–9.

———. "Revelation and History in J. C. K. von Hofmann." *Lutheran Quarterly* 10 (August 1958) 195–216.

———. "Unsere Stellung zum Sozialismus." *Badezeitung und Anzeiger für das Nordseebad Norderney*. March 1925.

———. "Die Wirkung Basilius' des Grossen auf das Mönchtum seiner Zeit." ThD diss., Philipps-University Marburg, 1928.

———. "Die Wirkung Basilius' des Grossen auf das Mönchtum seiner Zeit." Abbreviated diss., Georg August University of Göttingen, 1929.

Leo Ellis, Anne. "Last Stop, Prickly Pear." Unpublished manuscript, New York, 2010.

Lindemann, Gerhard. "Typisch jüdisch." In *Die Stellung der Evangelische-lutherische Landeskirche Hannovers zu Antijudaismus, Judenfeindschaft und Antisemitismus 1919–1945*. Schriftenreihe der Gesellschaft für Deutschlandforschung 63. Berlin: Duncker & Humblot, 1998.

Lindemann, Ilsetraut. *Von Assmann bis Wöberking: Stadtgeschichte in Straßennamen*. Bramsche: Rasch, 1985.

Maßner, Joachim. "Paul Friedrich Leo." In *Biographisches Handbuch zur Geschichte der Region Osnabrück*, edited by Rainer Hehemann, 180–81. Osnabrück: Rasch, 1990.

Meyer, Hermann. *Chronik der Kirchengemeinde St. Michaelis Eversburg*. Unpublished manuscript. Osnabrück, 1961.

Meyer, Philipp, ed. *Die Pastoren der Landeskirchen Hannovers und Schaumburg-Lippes seit der Reformation*. Göttingen: Vandenhoek & Ruprecht, 1942.

Oberlaender, Franklin. *Wir aber sind nicht Fisch und nicht Fleisch: Christliche "Nichtarier" und ihre Kinder in Deutschland*. Opladen: Wiesbaden, 1996.

Panayi, Panikos. "Victims, Perpetrators and Bystanders in a German Town: The Jews of Osnabrück Before, During and After the Third Reich." *European History Quarterly* 33 (2003) 451–92.

"Paul Leo: The Advocate for the Jews, 1893–1958." The Mendelssohns Society, n.d. https://www.mendelssohn-gesellschaft.de/en/mendelssohns/biografien/paul-leo.

Pauluhn, Ingeborg. *Zur Geschichte der Juden auf Norderney: Von der Akzeptanz zur Desintegration. Mit Dokumenten und historischen Materialien.* Oldenburg: Igel Wissenschaft, 2003.

Perels, Joachim. "Richard Karwehl—ein lutherischer Pfarrer aus dem Geist Karl Barths." *Jahrbuch der Gesellschaft für Niedersächsische Kirchengeschichte* 102 (2004) 161–75.

Rademacher, Michael. *Wer war wer im Gau Weser-Ems: Die Amtsträger der NSDAP and ihre Organisationen in Oldenburg, Bremen, Ostfriesland sowie der Region Osnabrück-Emsland.* Hamburg: LIBRI Druck and Vertrieb, 2000.

Rädisch, Wolfgang. *Die Evangelisch-lutherische Landeskirche Hannovers und der preußische Staat 1866–1885.* Hildesheim: August Lax, 1972.

Reese, Hans-Jörg. *Bekenntnis und Bekennen: Vom 19. Jahrhundert zum Kirchenkampf in der nationalsozialistischen Zeit.* Göttingen: Vandenhoeck & Ruprecht, 1974.

Rocker, Leif. "Der Umgang der Landeskirche Hannovers mit den 'getauften Juden' während der NS-Zeit." Examination paper, University of Göttingen, 2018. https://www.academia.edu/37118202/Der_Umgang_der_Landeskirche_Hannovers_mit_den_getauften_Pfarrern_während_der_NS_Zeit.

Röhm, Eberhard, and Jörg Thierfelder. *Juden – Christen – Deutsche.* Volume 3/I, *1938–1941*; and Volume 3/II, *1938–1941: Ausgestoßen.* Stuttgart: Calwer, 1995.

Rolffs, Ernst. *Evangelische Kirchenkunde Niedersachsens: Das kirchliche Leben in den Landeskirchen von Hannover, Braunschweig, Oldenburg und Schaumburg Lippe.* 2nd ed. Göttingen: Vandenhoeck & Ruprecht, 1938.

Salzmann, S. F. "The Theology of Wartburg Seminary." *Wartburg Seminary Quarterly* 17 (November 1954) 11–23.

Santayana, George. *The Life of Reason: Reason in Common Sense.* New York: Scribner's, 1905.

Schmidt, Kurt Dietrich, ed. *Die Bekenntnisse und gründsätzlichen Äusserungen zur Kirchenfrage des Jahres 1933/1934/1935.* Göttingen: Vandenhoeck & Ruprecht, 1934/1935/1936.

Simon, Bettina. "Ausgegrenzt, entrechtet, verraten. Paul Leo. Biographische Spuren-suche im Kontext des Verhaltens der ev.-luth. Landeskirche Hannovers (1933ff) gegenűber ihren Pastoren jűdischer Herkunft." Qualifying Paper under the Direction of Professor Eberhard Busch, University of Göttingen, 1996.

Simon, Christian. "Richard Karwehl (1885–1979). Der streitbare Pastor aus Osnabrück und sein Kampf gegen die hannoversche Kirchenleitung nach 1945." *Osnabrücker Mitteilungen* 99 (1994) 185–98.

Smid, Marikje. *Deutscher Protestantismus und Judentum 1932/1933*. Munich: Kaiser, 1990.

Solberg, Richard W. *Open Doors: The Story of Lutherans Resettling Refugees*. St. Louis: Concordia, 1992.

The Theological Declaration of Barmen. *Confessions of the Presbyterian Church U.S.A.* https://www.ekd.de/en/The-Barmen-Declaration-303.htm.

Wagner, Herbert. *Die Gestapo war nicht allein . . . Politische Sozialkontrolle und Staatsterror im deutsch-niederländischen Grenzgebiet 1929–1945*. Münster: Lit, 2004.

Weitkamp, Sebastian. "Hochmut und Fall: Die Schutzstaffel der NSDAP in Osnabrück 1932–1939." *Osnabrücker Mitteilungen* 113 (2008) 213–63.

———. "Der Sicherheitsdienst der SS– Eine Skizze." *Osnabrücker Mitteilungen* 112 (2007) 206–27.

Wolfes, Mathias. *Protestantische Theologie und moderne Welt*. Berlin: Walter de Gruyter, 1999.

Name Index

Subject Index